CW01509774

'In this accessible explc .... an's
fears, hopes and conv .... ape,
drawing deeply from th .... tice,
and making incisive con .... ence
and the wisdom Julian .... ody
and substance to a message of strength and reassurance too often
dismissed as trite or divorced from reality.'
The Revd Richard Stanton, priest director of the Julian Shrine, Norwich

'Like with the best of friends, Emma Pennington listens, cajoles, puzzles and rejoices with Mother Julian. We discover they both share in hope and yet both know about pain that will not go away. We learn that salvation in Christ is neither a sticking plaster nor an answer to a heavenly equation. Rather in Christ we find a revelation of one who truly salves both body and soul eternally. We learn this can genuinely sustain us in what too often or perhaps more often is a "troublous life". This is a compelling invitation to move from the shallows to the depths.'
The Very Revd David Monteith, dean of Canterbury

'Reading this book is an extraordinary encounter with a beautiful questioning holiness. Deep scholarship made elegantly accessible brings Mother Julian alive. The intensity of the experience of a mystic meets the questions of everyday life. The mystery of "all will be well" is integrated with a passion. It is a book that will help you grow in your faith and would be perfect for an Advent or Lent series in a church. Canon Pennington has written a scholarly devotional text that nestles right alongside the work of Henri Nouwen. Truly, read this book: you will find yourself on holy ground.'
The Very Revd Ian S. Markham PhD, dean and president of Virginia Theological Seminary and the president of The General Theological Seminary

'This is a beautifully written book which is both refreshing and original. In it, Julian's writings are interwoven with scripture and set within the devotional literature and landscape of the time, giving both rootedness and context. It is a book which is the fruit not only of careful study, but also of prayerful pondering and reflection. Emma has known CSMV over a number of years, and I'm delighted to commend *All Shall Be Well* both to those who are new to Julian of Norwich and those who wish to go deeper.'
Sister Elizabeth Jane CSMV, Community of St Mary the Virgin, Wantage

'A wonderful, carefully researched book, which combines an account of devotional practices current in medieval times with the relevance of Julian's teaching for people of today. Proposed as a spiritual director, Emma Pennington's Julian speaks straight to the heart as well as to the mind.'
Elizabeth Ruth Obbard ODC, Carmelite nun of Quidenham, and a writer and spiritual director

'Emma Pennington is a wise and insightful guide to the writings of Julian of Norwich. She invites us to make Julian our own spiritual companion as we seek to draw closer to God ourselves. Placing Julian in her wider context, she also enables us to see how her work was part of a broader tapestry of spiritual wisdom, which this book presents in fresh and illuminating ways. Not least, like Julian herself, Emma helps us face the challenges of faith lived out in a broken world, while also encouraging us to be a people of joyous hope and generous humanity.'
Andrew Braddock, dean of Norwich

'Having used Emma's last book so successfully as the Friends of Julian Lent Book, we're delighted to see this sequel completing, as it does, consideration of the revelations after Julian's striking change of focus in the middle of her account.'
Howard Green, secretary of the Friends of Julian of Norwich

ALL SHALL BE WELL

 Ministries

15 The Chambers, Vineyard
Abingdon OX14 3FE
+44(0)1865 319700 | brf.org.uk

Bible Reading Fellowship (BRF) is a charity (233280) and company limited by
guarantee (301324), registered in England and Wales

ISBN 978 1 80039 206 9
First published 2025
10 9 8 7 6 5 4 3 2 1 0
All rights reserved

Image acknowledgements listed on pp. 9–10.

A catalogue record for this book is available from the British Library

Printed by CPI Group (UK) Ltd, Croydon CR0 4YY

EMMA PENNINGTON

ALL SHALL BE WELL

VISIONS OF SALVATION WITH **JULIAN OF NORWICH**

Ministries

For Jonathan, who reminds me of what God's love is like, every day.

CONTENTS

THE FOURTEENTH REVELATION

THE FIFTEENTH REVELATION

THE SIXTEENTH REVELATION

LIST OF PLATES

between pages 128 and 129

PREFACE

It was 2019. Two years had passed since I had undergone the microvascular decompression operation to relieve the excruciating pain of trigeminal neuralgia (a condition that affects the nerve which transmits sensations of pain and touch from your face, teeth and mouth to the brain). Life had been transformed. No more pain to catch me unawares and trip me into the darkness of suffering. No more medication to fog my mind and constantly keep words at bay, like rare birds, known but not seen or held or spoken. No more silent, stealthy prohibitions to barricade food into a cage of inaccessibility. The prison bars had been left far behind, forgotten so quickly. Only with the crunch of an apple or crackle of a crisp would I suddenly remember these taboos that had now been broken and with the joy of freedom flew once more into the sky of gratitude.

It was 2019: a June day, a new house, a new city, a new job and a new start. I looked in the mirror in the bathroom, threw warm water over my face to gently cleanse the soft sleep away and, from the land of nightmares, the slightest electric touch rippled through my cheek. My will shone a light of defiance at its audacity. But the tiny ember of pain had not gone out and gradually over the following days and weeks it grew and grew into a slow burn that accompanied every word spoken and every morsel eaten. My pain was back, in a new form and in a new sensation, but back it was. There was to be no happy ending. All would not turn out to be well, after all.

All shall be well, all shall be well, and all manner of thing shall be well.

These are undoubtedly the best loved and most well known of Julian's words. They seem to have taken on a life of their own, being released from the page to appear on mugs, tea towels, plaques, cushions, notelets, posters, jewellery and T-shirts. Just as many of these items bring physical comfort, so Julian's famous words have brought hope and comfort to many – simple words that shine light into and on to the darkest of days and the most hopeless of situations. But what happens when all is not well, when pain and suffering return, when there is no solution to fix the problem, when there is no happy ending? What happens when all is not well with racial equality, not well with the future state of our planet, not well with social justice, not well with poverty, hunger, abuse and violence?

Perhaps surprisingly, this is the searching, questioning cry that Julian keeps returning to time and again, even as she gazes on the cross in joy and bliss. Only when she has pummelled Jesus with questions of how and why does he eventually reveal to her the heavenly meaning of his words 'All shall be well', a meaning which reaches beyond the trite and simplistic into the mystery of salvation, a mystery which once again draws the heart to Christ on the cross and invites us with Christ to delight in his love and joy; through which all shall be well, all shall be well, and all manner of thing shall indeed be well.

INTRODUCTION

REJOICING IN REDEMPTION

In 1373 a 30-year-old woman lay dying. As was the custom, her priest came to give her the last rites, and as he held a crucifix before her eyes, she saw it take on a 'common' light. The room darkened and from this cross a series of sixteen showings were given to the woman we now know as Julian of Norwich. Some of them focused on the events of the passion: the scourging of Christ, his crowning with thorns and his last pains of death. But others revealed the nature of God, his work of salvation and our relationship to him. For example, Julian describes her third revelation as showing 'that our Lord God, almighty wisdom, all love just as truly as he has made everything that is, so truly he does and works all things that are done'. In the fifth showing we see how the devil is overcome, and the sixteenth culminates with the revelation that hidden deep within the human soul:

> The blissful Trinity our maker, in Christ Jesus our Saviour, endlessly *wonyth* [dwells] in our soul, worshipfully ruling and governing all things, mightily and wisely saving us and keeping us for love.

Collectively she called these sixteen showings a revelation of love.

Julian lived through a time of great uncertainty, when the Black Death was raging through her world and there was civil unrest at home and wars abroad. It was also a time of dis-ease within the church, with church authority being questioned and practice reassessed. In her own anchoritic lockdown, she reflected on the revelations she had received on her deathbed in May 1373 for nigh on 20 years. The text which resulted from this time, often entitled by editors as *Revelations of Divine Love*, drew together an account of her visions along with her understanding of what she had seen of Christ's passion and her interpretation of the significance of his saving presence in our lives.

Of course, we would have known nothing of the events of this single day in May 1373 if Julian had not left us her writings. These consist in two forms: the short version and the long. The short text probably was written first, within about ten years of the event. It has a sense of immediacy to it which has not been dulled over time and focuses more on the description of the visions themselves along with her initial thoughts. The later text is about twice the length of the first. It is this text which we more often associate with Julian. We don't really know when it was written but we can have a good guess. Chapter 51, which recounts the example of a lord and a servant, does not appear in the short text and Julian tells us that she received this vision about 20 years after the initial revelation of love. Hence, we can date the long text to post 1393.

There is a strong argument put forward by Nicholas Watson, a well-known Julian scholar, that like William Langland, Julian never really completed a final version of her writing. Instead, she constantly returned to it, changing word order, adding in new observations and updating her ideas. In this sense Julian's work is not so much written for the purpose of 'publication' to an audience but is more of a spiritual exercise which became the focus of her outpouring of theological reflection and prayer. This notion rings true with the manner, style and tone of the long text, which is woven with thoughts that knot and unravel in thinking and interpretation. In *Revelations of Divine Love*, the reader is invited to enter a space of contemplative exploration where words are pushed to the very margins of sense and to discover there a deeper understanding and engagement with Christ.

Unfortunately, we have no definitive manuscripts which contain the original works. The short text is only found in the 15th century Amherst manuscript, whereas the earliest version of the entire long text can be found in the Paris Bibliothèque Nationale, known as the Paris manuscript. It is dated to post 1580 and seems to be a heavily altered version, missing many of the Middle English words that the later 17th century Sloane manuscript retains. This manuscript is known as S1 and is held by the British Library. a slightly later version, which appears to be a copy of S1, is also found in the British Library with further scribal additions and modernisations. This is known as S2.

Editors therefore mainly fall into two camps: those who follow Paris for its extra, perhaps more 'complete' text and those who use Sloane 1, feeling the importance of retaining the 'original' Middle English wording. Either way, at best, we only have copies of copies of her complete original work. Being a Middle English student and having first been introduced to Julian in the English faculty, I lean towards S1. This book therefore uses S1 as its base text, with my own translation, but I have also retained some of the Middle English words where they are of significance.

In addition, there are some compilation manuscripts which contain extracts of the text, namely the Westminster fragments and Upholland manuscript. They give us an idea that though Julian's text was possibly not widely circulated, it was still seen by a minority of religious in the 17th century as being part of an important group of writings which could assist them in their contemplative life of prayer. This group includes works by Walter Hilton, Richard Rolle and *The Cloud of Unknowing* author, writers who have come to be known as the English Mystics. The text of *Revelations of Divine Love* only really came to the attention of the modern audience at the beginning of the 20th century with Grace Warrack's edition of the short text from the Amherst manuscript. Since then, Julian's writings have become enormously popular.

Revelation of love

Of the sixteen showings that make up Julian's revelation of love, seven of them are rooted in the gospel narrative of the passion: the crowning of thorns; Christ on the cross; the scourging and mocking; the thirst of Jesus; Christ's words to the thief; the piercing of his side; and Mary at the foot of the cross. The biblical narrative may underpin them, but these seven showings soon pass from the word of scripture to personal encounter with the Word himself through revelation. Given the age in which Julian was living and the critical events of plague, suffering and death that were experienced, it's not surprising that in the first five showings it is the suffering human Jesus who we are brought before, as they linger on the pain of the passion and the slow process of his dying. These are explored in my first book, *At the Foot of the Cross with Julian of Norwich* (BRF Ministires, 2020).

With the ninth revelation, however, the tone changes markedly as the passion revelations become a springboard to contemplate salvation and our own personal relationship with Christ our Saviour that has been made accessible through his suffering on the cross. Increasingly, Julian hears the words of Jesus as he relates the salvation he brings to the ordinary experiences and struggles of faith. These are as relevant to us today as they were to the 'mine even Cristen' (the ordinary, lay believer) of the 14th century. It is out of this dialogue with Jesus that Julian explores, challenges and questions his words to her that 'all shall be well'. To fully understand and appreciate the significance of this single conversation, though, which ranges over many chapters of *Revelations of Divine Love*, it is important to place it within the scheme of the last seven showings. As you will see from below, the thirteenth revelation, which holds the beginning of this debate, sits in the midway point of these so-called visions of salvation. Showings ten to twelve build up to an ecstatic vision of Christ as Saviour, but then the clouds of sin obscure this reality. The rest of the showings unfold the reasons why this may be and how we can live trusting and knowing that hidden, beyond the veil, indeed all is well. The showings are as follows:

- the tenth revelation – the wounds of Christ leading to his cloven heart
- the eleventh revelation – the figure of Mary at the foot of the cross
- the twelfth revelation – the vision of Christ as our Saviour
- the thirteenth revelation – Christ's words of hope and reassurance that even in the midst of darkness and suffering 'all shall be well'
- the fourteenth revelation – united to God through prayer
- the fifteenth revelation – patient suffering
- the sixteenth revelation – the city of God within the soul.

The sequence of these seven showings takes us on a journey across a landscape which moves upward through confident visions of salvation, then descends into the reality of sin and reasoned debate on how all could be well, to end in a panoramic perception of the hidden work of Christ within the soul, undergirding and inspiring our everyday lives. This book embarks on that journey and through the individual chapters takes us through the highs and lows of Julian's revelatory landscape so that we may fully understand and thereby come to trust Jesus' words of reassurance.

The first three showings form an interlinking group within the one revelation of love. They follow one after another through chapters 24–27 in the long text of *Revelations of Divine Love*. For Julian they seemed to flow seamlessly into each other, like watching a moving tableaux or single take in a film. But our experience of them within her text is more disjointed as Julian sets them out as signs and waymarkers which open up different areas of thought. Around them she weaves her reflections and interpretation, the product of her deep contemplation of them.

The tenth and eleventh showings still have the sense of springing from the passion narrative, with the former seeming to focus on the moment when the lance pierced Jesus' side as he hung on the cross and the latter on Mary at the foot of the cross. But both of them quickly move from visions of the passion to a contemplation of salvation. For example, the tenth vision takes us not only to the wound of the lance but also into the gash in Jesus' side to find a place where all shall be safe, where we are nurtured and sustained by the blood flowing from the cloven heart of Christ. Similarly, the eleventh vision begins with a subtle scriptural reference to Mary as Christ looks down his right side to where she stood at the foot of the cross. But again, the mode of reading Julian's visions is disrupted as the showing soon develops and transmutes in form and style into a singular showing of the life of Mary and the manner in which she is the icon and exemplar not only of a contemplative, but also of all who are saved. These two visions therefore act in terms of a transition which shifts our imaginary frame from visions of the passion to salvation, from suffering to joy, from sorrow for sins to new life as the redeemed.

Increasingly the voice of Jesus becomes more and more prevalent. From only a few words in the ninth showing it becomes the very substance of the twelfth. This vision is perhaps the most ecstatic of all these later visions as Christ reveals to Julian who he is and the nature of his relationship with her and with us. Using short repetitive phrases, Julian seeks to express the ecstatic mode of this vision. Heaping them one upon another until she stretches language to such an extent that its descriptive ability dissolves and she is at a loss what to say. We are left with the hope that perhaps in this lifetime we too may have this experience as far as we are able.

With these two visions we see how Julian has been disrupted in the way she has read the showings so far, from interpreting and observing an outer bodily vision, which sought to evoke compassion for the suffering of Christ on the cross, to an inner 'ghostly' encounter with the person of Christ himself. In this new mode of showing, he speaks words which reveal both his glory and give pastoral reassurance that 'all is well'. Through her writing, Julian takes us to this point of contemplative encounter or 'noughting', where the discursive, reasoning nature of words can no longer function. We, along with Julian, find ourselves in that place of unknowing, of luminous darkness, of which both the *Cloud* author and Walter

Hilton speak, where we may know and encounter Christ in and for himself alone.

The twelfth vision is the high point or mountain peak of Julian's visionary experience. From glorious words spoken in terms that echo the Lord speaking from the burning bush to Moses, Julian then descends into the everyday experiences and trials of faith. In familiar conversation with Jesus she questions and explores why it is that our vision of Christ is so marred and distorted. Why did he allow sin? His gentle words that sin has its place but that 'all shall be well' are cold comfort to Julian. Over many chapters, she argues and questions Jesus over and over again, as she intellectually grapples with their meaning in the face of church teaching. Julian may fear that her argumentative style was bordering on impertinence, but the fact that she has such an intense and personal debate with Jesus shows how his passion has opened up a new familial relationship with God. It is a relationship comprised of mutual love and respect, where conversation can be open, mistakes held, fears allayed and trust embraced, rather than one of fear at speaking out to a wrathful father.

Into this space Julian considers two ways Jesus' assurance to her that 'all shall be well' are revealed. The first is the nature of prayer in the fourteenth vision. Here she sees that, however we feel or however many doubts we have about our prayers being heard, we are deeply and profoundly *onyd*, or united, to God through Christ, who is the 'ground of our beseeching'. The following showing then confronts the eternal problem of suffering and reveals that, in the light of the eternal assurances by Jesus that 'all shall be well', sin could have its place, its role and be 'behovely', or fitting, to the eschatological scheme of salvation. Though we live in a world of suffering, sin and pain, all is not what it seems. There is a deeper, spiritual reality, just beyond the veil, in which we can trust and to which we can be pulled at any moment as a child springing from the mire of sin. Each of these visions arises from a pastoral concern and each results in a vision of reassurance that God is 'our maker, our keeper, our lover', who is ever working to the end that 'all shall be well'.

The visions culminate in the sixteenth showing, which Julian understood to be the conclusion of all that had gone before. It shows the standard biblical image of Christ seated within the city of the soul on the throne of the heart, but given all the visions that have gone before, it becomes a powerful reminder of what salvation means, even when we cannot understand or experience it in everyday life. Julian draws on all the tropes and images of her time but re-envisions them in her showings of salvation so that Christ is not disengaged or apart, judging his creation with wrath and fury, but, like a mother, is a constant in our lives – nurturing, healing, answering our questions, casting out our fears and doting on us with love. The Trinity is ever secretly working to ensure that all is well, even though this may be hidden from us for a time.

Visions of salvation with Julian

Despite the difference in time, the complication of the medieval text and the convoluted language, Julian draws us time and again into her text to contemplate with her the wonder of God's love which was revealed in the sixteen showings that made up the one revelation of love. Julian constantly returned to her writing, not as a fastidious editor, but as a lover of God, to further reflect upon the truths she had seen and the reassurance they gave. For us, her writing thereby becomes a text that one lives with and refers to, pondering it in snippets and contemplating God through it daily.

Like Julian, this book ever seeks to point away from itself to the text and time of Julian so that you may return to her words with new eyes and deeper understanding. It does not wish to replace Julian's words but to allow her words to unfold for you, to find the mystery and revelation within. The book therefore consists of two parts. The first part places Julian within the context of her time and the devotional landscape in which she lived and wrote. It specifically considers the two aspects of her life which would have shaped her spiritual and pastoral questions and concerns, namely her relationship with the church and her role as a spiritual director within the community of Norwich.

In the second part we set out on our visionary journey with each chapter being staging posts along the way: the wound of Christ which leads to his cloven heart; the person and role of Mary at the foot of the cross; Christ as our Saviour; the promise that despite sin 'all shall be well'; God as the ground of our beseeching; the child rising from the swollen mass of sin; and the throne of Christ within the city of the soul. The biblical basis for Julian's vision is explored and the deeper meaning of her vision revealed as we, like Julian, search for the answer of how all can be well when it is so obviously not the case. This is set within the rich devotional context of the time in order to more fully understand the significance of Julian's interpretation of her visions and spiritual insight. Each chapter concludes with a guided reading exercise to enable you to enter the silence within Julian's words, with questions for personal devotion or discussion, and with a verse of scripture for the journey ahead.

So I invite you to set out with me on this quest to find the truth, the secret, whereby we can know and live in the reality that 'all indeed is well'.

PART I

− 1 −

DAUGHTER OF THE CHURCH

At the end of the Sloane 1 manuscript of *Revelations of Divine Love*, you will find this scribal addition to the text:

> I pray Almighty God that this book come not but into the hands of those that will be his faithful lovers, and to those that will submit themselves to the faith of 'holy church' and obey the sound understanding and teaching of the men that be of virtuous life, mature years and profound learning; for this revelation is deep theology and great wisdom, wherefor it may not dwell with him who is in thrall to sin and to the devil. And beware that you take not one thing after your affection and liking and leave another, for that is the way of a heretic. But take each thing along with everything else and truly understand that all is according to holy scripture and grounded in the same and that Jesus our true love, light and truth shall reveal this wisdom concerning himself to all pure souls who ask for it humbly and perseveringly. And you, to whom this book will come, thank our Saviour Christ Jesus, intently and with all your heart that he vouchsafed these showings and revelations of his endless love, mercy and goodness for you and to you, so as to be your and our safe guide and safe-conduct to everlasting bliss – which may Jesus grant us. Amen.

We cannot say for certain when this passage was added to the text, but it is clear that it was present in the manuscript by the time Sloane 1 was being copied out by the nuns of Cambrai in the 1650s.

The fact that it is there, even on only one of the manuscripts, raises some interesting questions as to how the text was to be read and who was allowed to read it. Julian's *Revelations of Divine Love* is clearly seen by someone as a dangerous text which has the potential to go against the teachings of the 'holy church'. Julian herself was aware that some of her questioning of Christ over his statement that 'all shall be well' bordered on impertinence, while it is clear that she struggles to hold the teachings of 'holy church' in light of her revelation especially on how God views the sinful with 'pity and not blame'. The questions which this raises about the nature of Julian's relationship with the church and why someone felt the need to add an injunction to her writing is what we will explore in this chapter.

Scribal warnings

Julian's *Revelations of Divine Love* is not the only text to contain such an injunction. Similar words of warning can also be found to open and close *The Cloud of Unknowing*, another English mystical text of the late 14th century. But these were written by an annonymous Carthusian author, primarily to inform those who may come to read it or pass it on to another that this text can only really be understood and be of use to those who had undertaken the highest form of contemplative life. To anyone else or to someone who did not read it through to the end, it could lead them into error. It's not a book for worldly chatters or the merely curious but only for those who have sought to be a perfect follower of Christ. The *Cloud* author thereby sets the tone of his book and prepares the reader to step carefully, for his text is holy ground. There is mention that some parts of his writing could lead someone into error through lack of understanding and cherry-picking of the ideas in the text. This kind of casual reader could fall into error if they do not approach his teaching with the utmost seriousness and desire to learn all he has to teach of deep contemplation.

This is very different from the scribal injunction added to Julian's text. Firstly, it's not written by the author. Though the tone of parts of the addition reflects Julian's revelations, it's clear that this is not written by Julian herself. Secondly, it comes at the very end of the text rather than at the beginning. The scribe is not aiding the reader in how they are to approach this text but rather seeking to dictate who it is to be passed on to. In many ways he is censoring the distribution of Julian's writing and seeking to limit it to only those 'who submit themselves to the faith of holy church'. As he states, the reason for this is that the revelation it describes is 'deep theology and great wisdom' and if it is not read in the light of scripture and as a whole it could be manipulated in heretical ways. This injunction, as opposed to that found at the beginning and end of *The Cloud*, is not so much about right learning but more about restriction and concern for heretical beliefs that this text could inspire.

A dutiful daughter

From her writing it seems clear that, though Julian struggles with the teachings of holy church in light of her revelation, she was a very pious and dutiful daughter of the church. In her short text she tells us how she 'desired three graces by the gift of God'. The first is to have intense recollection of Christ's passion; the second, a bodily sickness; and the third, to receive the gift of three wounds: contrition, compassion and longing for God. In each case she relates or grounds these gifts in the teaching of 'holy church'. In the first instance she tells us that she wishes to have bodily sight of the suffering of Christ on the cross but adds a disclaimer:

Notwithstanding this I truly believed in all the suffering of Christ in the manner in which holy church shows and teaches and also the paintings of crucifixes that are made by the grace of God, after the teaching of holy church to the likeness of Christ's passion, as far as man's wit may reach, notwithstanding all this true belief, I desired a bodily sight.

It was not until the 1380s that veneration of images was increasingly debated and highlighted as a sign of orthodoxy in the face of the Lollard denial. This radical movement openly protested against many of the practices and teachings of the church, including baptism and confession as necessary for salvation. The laity who followed it also called for scripture to be translated from Latin into English and advocated the teaching of women. Perhaps Julian felt this nod to orthodoxy was no longer necessary in later years, as she erases this reference from her long text.

Julian also deletes from her longer version her justification for asking for three wounds. In the earlier short text, she describes how a man of the church told her the story of St Cecilia. This legend recounts the life of the third-century virgin martyr who was forced to marry a pagan, Valerian, by her parents. He was converted to Christianity after seeing a vision of the angel of the Lord who watched over Cecilia and crowned her with a garland of roses. She and her husband were martyred at the hands of the Roman prefect. Cecilia received three blows to the neck from a sword, but these wounds failed to kill her, and it was believed that she preached the gospel for three days until she eventually died. This legend was very popular during the late 14th century and is told by the nun to the pilgrims as they travelled to Canterbury in Chaucer's *Canterbury Tales*.

While this desire for three wounds was common for any pious child of the time, Julian was aware that her wish for bodily sickness surpassed the 'common course of prayers', so she adds a condition to both this desire and her wish to have bodily sight of the passion, which echoes the words of Christ at Gethsemane:

Lord, you know what I wish. If it be your will that I have it, then grant it to me. And if it is not your will, good Lord, be not displeased, for I desire nothing except as you will.

Julian tells us that both these conditional desires passed from her mind, and while she outlines the three wounds in the long text, gone is the longer reference to the legend of St Cecilia. These changes to the short text reveal that in her later years Julian no longer felt it necessary to justify her childhood wishes. This reflects a more general tone of confidence that we find in the long text which no longer includes these references back to the teaching of 'holy church'. Perhaps one of the reasons for this may be that Julian's own religious standing in her community had changed and she now writes her longer version of her text while holding the prestigious office of an anchoress.

The anchoritic tradition

The term anchoress or anchorite comes from the Greek, meaning to withdraw. This solitary life goes back to the Desert Fathers and Mothers of the third century, but we also have a strong tradition in the UK with Guthlac of Crowland towards the end of the seventh century and Wulfric of Haselbury in the twelfth. It wasn't until the 13th century that this singular lifestyle took off, and it's from this period that we have our largest body of anchoritic texts, written for those who sought the enclosed life. These give us an insight into their lives, especially the *Ancrene Wisse,* or *Rule for Anchoresses*, which outlines how an anchoress is to live and pray in very practical detail, as well as an inner rule that should shape her thoughts and dedication to Christ. While we cannot be sure that this rule was followed as rigidly as is suggested, it does give us a good insight into a world largely unknown to us today. It's also from this rule that we get the idea of Julian's cat, as the rule states that an anchoress couldn't keep a cow but was allowed a cat. Whether Julian actually had a cat I'm afraid we cannot say for sure, as she makes no mention of it.

During the 14th century many anchoress cells were attached to the side of the parish church rather than being isolated places in the wilds. A few of these still remain, including the anchoress cell at Holy Trinity, Skipton. For others there are only the windows into the church or a plaque on the wall to show where they had once been. This is the case for Christine Carpenter's cell at Shere church in Surrey (see Plate 1). Notably, the church of St Julian was bombed during the war and the anchoress' cell has been reconstructed on the site where the original foundations are believed to be.

The anchoritic life

It was a big undertaking by a parish as well as an anchoress to be incarcerated into a room on the side of the local church. There, of course, had to be enough money to keep her for the rest of her life and she often required a servant to attend to her needs. In a will of 1404, there is a bequest made to Julian which refers to a maid called Sarah and then in 1415 to another called Alice. But the solitary life may well not have been the harsh life that we always associate with an anchoress or as depicted in the 1993 film of the same name. The anchoress came directly under the auspices of the bishop, and there is evidence which shows that this was taken very seriously by the episcopate. A *Provinciale* (a collection of provincial statutes) of the early 15th century reflects the nature of this relationship. It demonstrates the responsibility the bishop had in, firstly, investigating the suitability of the candidate, then in ensuring that there was adequate financial support, in addition to examining the suitability of the anchorhold.

The prospective anchoress also needed to give proof of her calling to this life, and it's possible that the short text of the *Revelations of Divine Love* forms the basis of such a document. Once permission was given and provision made, the bishop conducted the service of the dead and entombed the anchoress in her cell for life, a moment which is depicted in the lovely 14th-century manuscript in the Parker Library,

Corpus Christi College, Cambridge (see Plate 2). But the involvement of the bishop did not end there, for it was also his responsibility to supervise the anchoress and ensure her orthodoxy and spiritual success. The anchoress can be seen as less of a troublemaker on the fringes of the church and more like a pillar of the establishment who was honoured and trusted to uphold the teachings of 'holy church' and guide the flock in spiritual care in addition to the parish priest who held ultimate pastoral cure of souls.

Anchoritic renown

By the late 14th century this way of life had become very popular, with 24 anchorites or anchoresses attached to churches in Norwich alone. They may have been costly to keep, but they also gave kudos to a local parish church. It was very possible that Julian herself was well known at the time, at least in and around Norwich. The short text begins with a scribal addition which not only identifies the author but also locates the manuscript to a place and a time:

> Here is a vision, showed by the goodness to a devout woman. And her name is Julian, who is a recluse in Norwich and still alive, AD1413. In this vision there are many comforting words and greatly stirring words for those who desire to be Christ's lovers.

The second sentence at least enables us to date this scribal addition to 1413, if not the copy of the short text itself. Its addition gives us a vital piece of information which we would not otherwise have known, namely that Julian had received her revelations in 1373, let alone written this amazing work by 1413. The fact that the scribe includes it therefore suggests that he certainly knew of her in her day.

There is very little external evidence about Julian's life. One vital reference can be found in the *Book of Margery Kempe,* written in the 1430s just up the road from Norwich at King's Lynn. In chapter 18

Margery describes the people she goes to see in Norwich for spiritual guidance. One of these is the vicar of St Stephen's, who becomes her confessor; another is the White Friar William Southfield, who also gives her spiritual counsel and supports her in the face of fierce opposition from the church authorities. Finally, the Lord commands her to go and see 'an anchoress in the same city who is called Dame Julian' and who has a reputation for being an expert in revelations and giving good advice. It is clear from this singular reference that, though we have little documentary evidence about Julian's life as an anchoress, she was certainly well known and respected in the city of Norwich.

Revelatory doubts

Despite Julian's position within the church and local community, her text reveals a need to claim that her revelation is consistent with church teaching. She even, like Margery, has doubts about the authenticity of her vision as she reveals in chapter 66 of the long text:

> Then a member of a religious order came to me and asked me how I fared, and I said I had raved all day and he laughed loud and heartily. And I said, 'The cross that stood before my face, methought it flowed with blood.' And with this word, the person that I spoke to waxed woe and marvelled, and anon I was sore ashamed and astounded by my recklessness. And I thought, 'This man takes seriously the least word I might say yet knows no more about it than that.'

As a result of the response by the friar or canon, Julian is full of shame and wishes to confess her folly at saying she had received a revelation, but she feels unable to tell a priest, for it would show that she also doubted what God had revealed to her. Julian tells us that she is caught in a wretched state between doubting her revelation and doubting God, which results in her losing the comfort which her revelation had given her.

Julian falls asleep and, as dreams so often do, her conflict and doubts are visualised as something else. In Julian's case, it is in the appearance of a devil who tries to throttle her. It is only then that Julian realises what has happened and:

> Anon I accepted what our Lord had shown me that very day, with all the faith of holy church – for I beheld it is both one – and fled thereto as my comfort. And immediately all vanished away, and I was brought to great peace and rest without bodily sickness or a troubled conscience.

Julian is reassured that her revelations are true and do not go against the teaching of the church.

Assertions of orthodoxy

Throughout her text, Julian holds on to this fundamental belief that her revelation showed nothing contrary to the teaching of 'holy church'. She states this emphatically early on in her later longer text, replacing an apology for being a woman who dares to write about a revelation with this confident address:

> I speak to those who will be saved, for at this time God showed me no others. But in all things, I believe as holy church preaches and teaches. For the faith of holy church which I had beforehand understood and, as I hope, by the grace of God willfully kept in use and custom, stood continually in my sight, understanding and meaning, never to receive anything that might be contrary to it. And with this intent I beheld the showing with all diligence, for in all this blessed showing I behold it as one in God's meaning.

Similar assertions occur throughout her long text, which raises the question: who is Julian trying so hard to convince of her orthodoxy?

There are certainly aspects of Julian's revelation which she finds hard to reconcile with the teaching of 'holy church'. The most important of which is her showing concerning how God sees sin and the words of Christ that 'all shall be well'. While these words bring comfort to many today, for Julian, in the late 14th century, they are profoundly problematic. Contrary to the Augustinian understanding of sin and the final judgement, Julian's revelation teaches that God does not look upon sinners with wrath and that in heaven even the scars from the wounds of sin will become to us badges of glory and honour. Similarly, the church's doctrine on hell, which was fearsome and pervasive, is dismissed, as Jesus reassures Julian that 'all shall be well', hinting at the idea of universal salvation. The incongruity between these conflicting teachings deeply troubled Julian, who was also writing and adapting her text during a time of religious unrest and when she even risked accusations of heresy.

Church criticism

Throughout the history of the temporal body of Christ, the church, there have been those who questioned and dissented against the authority of the church at the time. Even the early church invariably worked out what it believed through fierce debates and controversies. The church of the 14th century was not immune to such crises. We often think of the Reformation of the 16th century as the great turning point between the medieval and early modern world of the church, but it had its beginning in the 14th century. For at that time there was dis-ease about church power, the intermediary role of clergy and sacraments, the interpretive control and exclusivity of scripture, and the degradation of church structures and morals. Such concerns were beautifully expressed by William Langland's personification of 'holy church' in his poem *Piers Plowman*.

Like Langland, Julian expresses a similar concern that the mechanisms to handle sin, namely confession and penance, are unable to alleviate a sense of sinfulness and give assurance of forgiveness. Julian also gently, if courageously, challenges the attitude towards the teaching role of women in the church:

> Even though I am a woman, ought I therefore believe that I should not tell you of the goodness of God, since I saw that at the same time that it is his will that it be known.

Such internal questioning and criticism by people like Julian and Langland escalated in the 1380s and culminated in the Lollard movement.

Religious unrest and heresy

An important figure in this religious dissent, if not the initiator, was the Oxford scholar John Wycliffe, who openly preached against the corruption of the church and wrote numerous tracts and books dismissing the key doctrines of the church in his day. He was also seminal in translating the Bible into English for the first time. At the Council of Blackfriars in 1383 a number of his propositions were denounced as heretical and condemned, but such was the church's ability to contain such alternative radical thinking that Wycliffe was neither excommunicated nor denied his living, as many were in sympathy with his criticism of the church, not least the king. It was only later, in 1415 at the Council of Constance, that Wycliffe was declared a heretic and his writings banned. This was part of a clampdown by church authorities who, as a response to the unrest, tightened up their teachings on the authority of the church, including the role of women in teaching. Anyone who was seen to have Lollard sympathies was rooted out and some even ended up by being burnt at the stake. Julian seems to be making an oblique reference to these religious troubles of her day when she writes:

> Holy church shall be shaken in sorrow and anguish and tribulation in this world as men shake a cloth in the wind.

In this atmosphere of dis-ease, devotional figures like Margery Kemp came under suspicion. She was brought before the church authorities for following so-called Lollard tendencies numerous times but was never convicted. Her book is often seen as a justification and validation of her unconventional devotional life, which during those nervous years of the late 14th and early 15th centuries could easily be seen as flouting church teaching. In this context Julian's statements of orthodoxy have been interpreted as mere posturing to enable her to escape accusations of heresy. This could easily be said of Julian's text if she did not seem to be so concerned with the seeming incongruity of certain aspects of her revelation with the teaching of 'holy church' herself, in particular the words of Christ in her thirteenth showing that 'all shall be well'.

Re-envisioning church teaching

Julian's answer to this incongruity is on one level to 'hold steadfastly to the faith as I had previously understood and at the same time that I should believe that all things shall be well, as our Lord revealed at that time' – in a sense, to hold the two truths in tension until the great deed of the Lord at the end time.

On another level, however, Julian also seeks throughout her text to re-envision her understanding of church teaching as a consequence of her revelation, thereby allowing the light of the showing to inform her beliefs in the church. A good example of this can be seen in her teaching on prayer.

In chapter 6 of the long version of *Revelations of Divine Love,* Julian re-envisions her understanding of the many liturgical feasts which had become commonplace by the end of the 14th century. This section directly follows Julian's spontaneous prayer, which closes chapter 5 and arises from her vision of the littleness of creation and our need to be noughted to know that God is all we need:

God, of your goodness give me yourself, for you are enough for me and I may ask for nothing that is less, that will be full worship of you. And if I ask anything less, then I am always in want, but only in thee do I have all.

It is an ecstatic response to her revelatory encounter, and her text leads us up to this moment, whereupon reading her words we break forth into prayer and they become our words too.

The spontaneous moment of prayer ends, and, in the aftermath, Julian contemplates 'the custom of our prayers' – the ways in which, during her day, prayer has become mediated through many different feasts and devotions, praying through Christ's attributes or saints rather than praying directly to God:

We pray to God for his holy flesh and his precious blood, his holy passion, his dear worthy death and wounds and all the blessed kindness, the eternal life, and we receive all this because of his goodness; and we pray to him by the love of his sweet mother who bore him and all the help we have from her is because of his goodness; and we pray by the holy cross that he died on, and all the virtue and the help we have from the cross, it is because of his goodness.

Unlike the Lollards, who were deeply against praying to the saints or honouring images and feasts for the different aspects of Christ's passion, Julian does not so much criticise these means of prayer, but she reminds us of why they have been ordained. The means are not an end in themselves; they are only given so that we may seek, understand and know the goodness of God. In this statement there is an implicit adaptation of how feasts, images and intermediary devotional methods are to be used. Her revelation has reminded Julian of why God has given them to the church. They are to be conduits of grace and goodness not to be loved in themselves, for that would be idolatry. In this way Julian's revelation does not so much alter the teachings of 'holy church' as bring a deeper understanding and spiritual awareness that they already contained. Instead, she re-envisions the practice so that it reflects once more the real teaching that has become hidden and in turn reveals the importance of her revelation, which enables the church to see its purpose and teaching once more from the perspective of God's love and goodness.

Julian's relationship with the church may be complex and contradictory, but it is through this re-envisioning of the church she loves and follows that a second scribe felt compelled to close Julian's manuscript not with words of injunction but rather in the form of a diminishing pyramid with this *encomium* to her and her vision:

Here ends the sublime and wonderful Revelations
of the unutterable love of God in Jesus Christ,
vouchsafed to a dear lover of his and in
her to all his dear friends and
lovers, whose hearts, like
hers, do flame in the
love of our
Dearest
Jesu

– 2 –

JULIAN THE SPIRITUAL DIRECTOR

We don't often think of Julian as a spiritual director. The reason for this is that she is invariably described as a mystic, an image which conjures up someone who is on the edge of society, separate and apart, uninterested, at odds even, with the life of the church. Julian scholarship has sought to question this perception and reassessed what it would have been like to be an anchoress in late 14th-century Norwich. Rather than being on the edge of society we find Julian situated within its very heart, fulfilling a vital role to the community as spiritual guide and pastoral aid. This is also very different from the image we have of an anchoress as being enclosed, withdrawn from the world and cocooned within a silent world of prayer, much like the little detached hut depicted in the Parker Library Manuscript (see Plate 2). However, this was not always the case. In this chapter we will explore Julian's role as a spiritual director and the way her text responds to the spiritual and pastoral concerns of her day.

The anchoress was allowed two windows, one into the church to see the celebration of the Eucharist and the other through which she could listen to the concerns of the people who came to her. The *Ancrene Wisse* warns the anchoress of the temptation of loving this window and turning it into a place of gossip, however 'holy' that might seem to be. Julian's cell was abutting the side of St Julian's church on one of the main thoroughfares into Norwich, so it is likely that she was kept very busy with the many people who came to her seeking guidance and support from the anchoress at St Julian's.

Two of Julian's visions, the fourteenth and fifteenth, directly address pastoral concerns that she must have heard and known about from her window, let alone experienced in her own spiritual life. In a recent play called *Cell*, writer and performer Cindy Oswin creates an immersive medieval soundscape which captures what Julian probably would have heard from her cell. Collating medieval sounds of street cries, carts, bells, music and plainsong, she reveals just how noisy it would have been and, rather than presenting a serene, disembodied Julian, the play explores how Julian struggled with her own internal noise of doubts and limitations within the bustle of a late-medieval city and having to deal with the demands of her community.

A visit from Margery Kempe

There's evidence to suggest that Julian was well regarded for her spiritual direction. As mentioned in the previous chapter, Margery Kempe recounts a visit she made to Julian in 1413. She is a good example of one of the pious laity of the late 14th century, who lived the kind of non-institutional devotional life which was increasingly popular at this time. Margery not only identifies herself with the great visionaries of the day, like Bridget of Sweden, but also writes a text in way of a defence and justification of her life. In this *Book of Margery Kempe*, she also describes the very vivid and narratorial visions she received in which she imaginatively takes part in key moments in Jesus' life. Margery is rather distrusted by the church authorities and doubted by the clergy, so in 1413 she goes to see Julian, the anchoress of Norwich:

> The afore said creature was much comforted both in body and soul by this good man's words and greatly strengthened in her faith. And then she was bidden by our Lord for to go to an anchoress in the same city who was called Dame Julian. And so she did and showed her the grace that God put in her soul of compunction, contrition, sweetness and devotion, compassion

with holy meditations and high contemplation and full many holy speeches and dalliances that our Lord spoke to her soul and many wonderful revelations which she showed to the anchoress to know if there was any deceit in them, for the anchoress was expert in such things and could give good counsel.

Book of Margery Kempe, book 1, chapter 18

This text gives us a wonderful window into why people sought out Julian and what she might have said to them at her window.

The first and perhaps most important point is that Julian's revelations were well known, and she had a reputation as being an anchoress who was 'expert in such things [namely revelations] and could give good counsel'. Margery gives no reference to a specific text, but this is not surprising as Julian and Margery lived in a primarily oral world in which ideas and information flowed through conversation and preaching rather than through the expensive medium of book production. Julian's text itself has been described as an echo chamber of allusions to theological ideas and images garnered from such an oral world. So it is through this medium that people would have known about her vision, if not the texts of her work.

Secondly, Margery has been told to seek out Julian because she wants advice and guidance as to whether these 'wonderful revelations' she has received are true or whether they are full of deceit and lies. She wants authentication from someone who is an expert in this area and also is well known for giving good advice. By this reference, it is clear that Julian has given spiritual guidance to many before Margery and has a reputation for the help she can provide. Margery goes on to paraphrase Julian's words to her, and we trust they are authentic to Julian, as they resonate with the language and ideas we have come to be familiar with in *Revelations of Divine Love*.

If you have given or received spiritual direction, then Julian's words may be comfortingly familiar as they give Margery some sound spiritual advice. She counsels Margery to be obedient to the will of God and fulfil what he places in her soul as long as it is not against the 'worship of God' but is 'profitable to his even Cristen'. For if it goes against this then it is not the making of a 'good spirit but an evil one'. In modern terms, we would recognise this statement as one of discernment. Because of his very nature, the Holy Spirit can only make a soul stable and steadfast in right faith and right belief, when he dwells within the temple of the spirit, namely the soul. If not, then Julian likens the soul to a sea which is unstable and unsteadfast, always blown about by the wind. Julian gives Margery the tools to discern when the Holy Spirit dwells within her and whether she is able to receive these gifts of God. Stability is one, but others are the tears of contrition, devotion and compassion. These are three of the catechetical markers which showed that a soul's repentance for sin was true and real, the stirring of God rather than the work of the devil.

Julian goes on to give biblical authority to her words by alluding to Romans 8:26, 'We do not know what we ought to pray for, but the Spirit himself intercedes for us through wordless groans', along with 2 Corinthians 6:16, 'We are the temple of the living God.' Julian also refers to Jerome, but the proverbial statement that 'tears torment the devil more than do the pains of hell' is more likely attributed to St Bernard in the Middle English *Speculum Christiani* than to the biblical commentator.

Julian ends her advice by praying that Margery may have two virtues: perseverance in the face of the spite, shame and reproof she receives from the world; and patience that she will trust her stirrings come from God. Julian thereby allays Margery's doubts and fears for the moment, but these fears were to beset Margery throughout her life. In this passage we have a unique insight into the concerns which beset a soul and what advice and guidance would have been given by an exemplary spiritual director of the time. It is clear that this visit was more than just an hour's conversation at a window, as Margery writes that they talked together for many days.

Two types of sickness

Julian's text also captures some of the other concerns that were brought to her window, and these reveal a similar sense of fear, but this time arising from a lingering dread even after confession. Chapters 73, 74 and 75 of *Revelations of Divine Love* are not widely read by those attending retreats or quiet days on Julian of Norwich. Yet they link in with Margery's doubts and fears about her spiritual gifts and reveal a more general dis-ease which weighs the soul down. Julian has been contemplating why it is that we cannot always see the loving gaze of the Lord and instead are blinded by our mortal earthiness and the darkness of sin. God shows her that there are two types of sickness which afflict us: impatience or sloth, and despair or doubting fear.

In a sense Margery exhibits both of these – a doubtful dread about her life and visions but also a restless impatience which calls for the gift of patience from Julian. In the context of the spiritual life, impatience was not just about wanting things to happen faster or being irritable; it held the sense of sloth, the monastic sin of *accidia*, which was defined as a state of listlessness or torpor, of not caring and being unable to pray or work. It was a sin particularly associated with the religious and most devout. It was also often understood as being the sin closest to despair, and in Dante's *Inferno* it is *accidia* which brings the poet to the gates of hell. These are the only two forms of sin that Julian sees in her vision, but they are the two which 'most tasks and torments us'.

Julian goes on to reveal in chapter 73 how this is experienced by the devout, namely, 'such men and women that for God's love hate sin and dispose themselves to do God's will', those who sought advice and guidance from Julian:

And of this knowing we are most blind; for some of us believe that God is all mighty and may do all, and that he is all wisdom and can do all, but that he is all love and will do all, there we stop. And this unknowing, it is this that most hinders God's lovers, as to my sight; for when we begin to hate sin and amend ourselves by the ordinance of holy church, yet there dwells a dread that hinders us, for the beholding of ourselves and of our sins done before, and sum of us for our everyday sins; for we hold neither our covenants nor keep our cleanness that our lord sets us in, but fall often in so much wretchedness that shame it is to see. And the beholding of this makes us so sorry and so downhearted that we can hardly find any comfort. And this dread we sometimes take for a meekness, but this is a foul blindness and weakness. And we cannot despise it as we do another sin that we know, for it comes from the enemy. And it is against the truth.

When this long text is placed alongside the shorter version it is interesting to note just how many additions and changes have been made. At the core of this passage is Julian's observation that the processes or ordinances of 'holy church' for dealing with sin, namely contrition, confession and absolution, are not enabling the devout to be released from their sense of sinfulness. Rather, even after confession, there remains a dread or fear that traps the person in a cycle of dwelling on themselves and their previous sins. In this long version of the text, Julian adds that not only does the soul dwell on past sins brought to confession but in our covenants, namely confession and baptism, we are compounding the problem and making the soul more conscious of the extent of sinfulness.

It seems that the short text was directed towards a particular group of people, contemplatives and the most devout, but now, in the long text, the problem is presented as a more universal concern, as the third person pronouns are altered to first person, which implies that Julian is including herself in this spiritual problem. So we see a shift from this scrupulosity and fear, affecting only contemplatives and the very devout, to a more general concern within the spiritual life. This shift probably occurred from Julian hearing the concerns of ordinary people and realising that more folk were suffering from a doubtful dread than just Margery and contemplatives.

The effects of this doubtful dread are also added to the short version of Julian's *Revelations of Divine Love*. Now she sees that it is this very fear which is turning the soul in on itself so that the soul is blinded and cannot know or see any comfort from the Lord. Margery presented this state when she arrived at Norwich, and it takes real discernment from Julian to point out to Margery not only what she is feeling in terms of restless impatience but also where it comes from. The reason being, as she points out in the passage above, is that such fear or dread is hard to discern for ourselves as it seems to be a meekness and therefore is difficult to easily scorn.

The problem of penance

Lying behind the problem of fear, which Julian articulates here in pastoral terms, is the sense that in the late 14th century the means of alleviating sin, namely the sacrament of penance, was increasingly incapable of doing so. Since the Fourth Lateran Council of 1215, when Pope Innocent III had stipulated that everyone should confess at least once a year, a body of legislation and texts of manuals had grown up to help parish priests fulfil their task of the cure of souls. Sin was seen in terms of a disease, a sickness which the medicine of confession could heal through a discerning physician, the priest. But increasingly, focus rested on the legitimacy of the confession, rather than on the words of absolution. Penitents were encouraged to make sure that their confession was full and complete. Such emphasis turned the eyes of the penitent inwards in a scrupulous way, and naturally they focused on the black and ingrained spots of sin, too numerous to be voiced in confession, rather than on the reassurance of sins forgiven.

William Langland encapsulates this perfectly in his poem *Piers Plowman* in the figure of Active Man, the everyman figure. Patience and Conscience have set out with the dreamer to find Piers Plowman. The manuals of confession are left far behind, as is Clergie and his books. They meet the figure Hawkin, who wears a coat soiled by the seven deadly sins, but Hawkin is unaware of these many spots of sin. Conscience then begins to teach him how to make his coat clean once again with contrition of the heart, confession of the mouth and satisfaction. In the speech that follows, Conscience exhorts Hawkin to acknowledge his shame. The section ends with a contrite Hawkin, who now realises the full extent of his sin: 'so harde it is....to *lyve* (live) and to do sin. *Synne serveth* us *evere* (Sin ever serves us)'. It is at this point that the dreamer Will awakes, leaving Hawkin aware of his sinful state but without any means to alleviate it. Penance had only brought the penitent to the point of knowledge that he is muddied by the stain of sin but had been inadequate to then deal with it.

It is this same concern that we find with Julian's *Revelations of Divine Love*. Spiritual souls are acutely aware of their sinfulness, but the ordinances of 'holy church' seem incapable of freeing them from this lingering dread of sin. What is the answer to this doubtful dread which seems to be afflicting many in their spiritual life? Well, instead of running away from the language and notion of fear into a singular theology of love and forgiveness, Julian enters into the issue head-on.

The four forms of fear

In chapter 74 of *Revelations of Divine Love*, Julian describes four forms of fear or dread which are similar to those found in other Middle English texts, such as *Contemplations of Love and Dread*. Through describing these forms, she helps the reader or listener to begin to discern for themselves, firstly, what is going on and why they feel fear, and secondly, what might be godly about this sense of fear and what is not. In this way she validates the lived experience of people in their spiritual life but also helps them understand how to navigate it into what is beneficial.

The first manner or form of dread is fear of attack. This is often likened to the sense of when someone cries 'Fire! Fire!', as is explained in the *Ancrene Wisse*. It is good insofar as it makes you aware of danger and your own vulnerability. So, it can purge or cleanse a soul that is sleeping in sin.

The second is fear of suffering, which again has the qualities of awakening the soul that sleeps in sin. It's this kind of fear that 'Doom' wall paintings and the Middle English text *Prick of Conscience* sought to evoke, not simply fear for fear's sake but in order to turn the soul to seek God. Julian even states that this fear is evoked by the Holy Spirit, who 'touches us' into contrition for our sins.

The third dread is very different: doubtful dread. Both dread of affray and dread of pain lead the soul towards God. But doubtful dread does the opposite and leads the soul away from God into despair. The only way this dread can be avoided or healed is by grace, through the true knowing of love which transforms the dread into love.

Finally, there is one dread which pleases God and that is 'reverent dread'. It is the kind of fear which is more akin to the silent wonderment of awe that brings us to our knees in consciousness of the divine. It is the dread which drew the shepherds and the wise men to the stable to see the Lord God Almighty, helpless in a feeding trough but destined for the rescue of God's world from darkness and fear. It is the kind of fear mentioned in Proverbs 9:10, 'The fear of the Lord is the beginning of wisdom, and knowledge of the Holy One is understanding', and Isaiah 11:3, 'He will delight in the fear of the Lord.'

Into this description of fear Julian brings the notion of love. Love and reverent dread are not seen as alien or hostile to each other but rather as brothers, two sides of the same coin which are gifted to us by grace. It is as appropriate for us to have awe and deep respect on account of the lordship of the Father as it is to love on account of his goodness and compassion. Throughout *Revelations of Divine Love,* Mary is presented by Julian as the definitive icon and forerunner of the person who displays this reverent dread: a dread which responded in amazement that the Lord should choose her to be the Mother of God; a dread which she invites troubled souls at her window to emulate so that they too may experience that deep love of the Lord revealed in his forgiveness and compassion for our fallen human state.

Woven into the fabric of her text, Julian's pastoral words of guidance reveal just how much of her enclosed life was spent listening and advising ordinary folk on their spiritual life. It is out of and into this forum of pastoral care and spiritual advice on living the life of the redeemed that Julian's visions speak. Julian may not be well known today for her skills in spiritual direction, but it is certainly through this dedication to her community that she comes to share the insights of her revelation with those of her day, along with us who read her words now.

PART II

THE TENTH REVELATION

– 3 –

THE WOUND OF CHRIST

The first vision on our journey takes us away from the suffering of Christ on the cross into the wound in his side to show that deep within the cloven heart of Christ there is a place where we are kept safe. We begin with the assurance that through Christ's passion all has been made well.

> Then with a glad countenance our lord looked into his side and beheld, rejoicing; and with his sweet gaze led the understanding of his creature into the same wound in his side. And there he showed a fair delightful place, large enough for all mankind that shall be saved to rest in peace and love.

In the tenth showing of her *Revelations of Divine Love*, Julian describes the person of Christ. It marks the transition from showings focused on the passion of Christ to visions of salvation. Gone is the passion with all its pain, gone is the suffering on the cross, gone is the slow dying we had to endure with Christ. Instead, we have entered beyond the veil into a place of deep and everlasting peace as, with a countenance of sheer joy, Christ looks down at the marks of his suffering and invites Julian to contemplate his wounds. Most significantly, to contemplate the wound that was caused by the spear piercing his dead body at the crucifixion, as recounted in John 19:34. The scene is also reminiscent of the resurrection narrative where Jesus invites Thomas to place his finger in Jesus' wound in order to believe. Jesus doesn't just invite Julian to look or to touch his wounds as he did Thomas. Rather, Jesus motions her to enter right into this gash made in his flesh. To a modern audience this can seem rather grisly and ghastly, more like a slasher movie than a serene contemplation of divine love. So, what is going on here?

As with many of Julian's visions, the language and imagery which she uses comes from deep within the devotional culture of the late 14th century. In this world biblical images and ideas were often conflated into purely visual tropes and markers which the devout would look at and then meditate upon. It was a multilayered experience which combined various biblical narratives into one image that would express the meaning behind the words, rather than the narrative events themselves. In many ways this is what is happening in her tenth revelation. Julian is not so much referring to the story of the passion or the resurrection, but creating a multidimensional image through her words which the reader is then able to explore at different levels in order to reflect on her vision of Christ, in order for us to be present before him in our own experience and lived reality. We can see this when we turn to consider the similarities that Julian's vision has to a popular devotional image of the late medieval period known as *Imago Pietatis* (Man of Sorrows). A version of this iconography is depicted in a French book of hours (a prayer book popular with lay people at the time) that dates from 1375, just a couple of years after Julian's revelations (see Plate 3).

The Man of Sorrows

The iconography of the Man of Sorrows has its basis in the great suffering servant songs found in the book of Isaiah. Christian commentators quickly associated these words of rejection and humiliation with the person of Christ and his suffering on the cross. Isaiah writes:

> He was despised and rejected by men; a man of sorrows, and acquainted with grief; and as one from whom men hide their faces he was despised, and we esteemed him not. Surely he has borne our griefs and carried our sorrows; yet we esteemed him

stricken, smitten by God, and afflicted. But he was wounded for our transgressions; he was crushed for our iniquities; upon him was the chastisement that brought us peace, and with his stripes we are healed.

ISAIAH 53:3–5 (ESV)

For the medieval world the devotional depictions of the Man of Sorrows encapsulated in a single image not only the biblical meaning of the idea, but also its association with the suffering of Christ for the person who meditated upon it. Just like Julian's vision of encounter, so the image on the right of this small miniature shows Jesus in his crucified form, naked above the waist, crowned with thorns and showing his still bleeding hands and side. His head hangs down to the right, echoing the drooping, dying and suffering of Christ as depicted in so many crucifixion scenes of this period. He also wears the same expression of deep agony as found in images of the passion at this time, an expression which sought to evoke a similar sense of deep sorrow and compassion in those who looked at him. Hence the devotional image of the Man of Sorrows resonates with many aspects of the passion devotions that were created to move the watcher to tears of empathy for the suffering humanity of Christ.

Alongside, and combined with these passion tropes, we also find the imagery of the resurrection. His downward glancing head not only represents Christ on the cross, but he also looks down in order to direct the attention of the onlooker to focus on the wound in his side. We move then through an image of the passion to an *aide memoir* for the resurrection narrative, where Thomas is invited to place his hands into the wounds in the gospel account of John:

Although the doors were locked, Jesus came and stood among them and said, 'Peace be with you.' Then he said to Thomas, 'Put your finger here, and see my hands; and put out your hand, and place it in my side. Do not disbelieve, but believe.'

Thomas answered him, 'My Lord and my God!' Jesus said to him, 'Have you believed because you have seen me? Blessed are those who have not seen and yet have believed.'

JOHN 20:26–29 (ESV)

While the devotional focus of the Man of Sorrows is invariably still in the sphere of evoking compassion, like all passion meditations, Julian's vision is anything but sorrowful. Instead, she opens her account of the tenth revelation with a description of the joyous demeanour of our Lord as he shows her his wounded side. This is echoed in the last words of the chapter, where Julian describes the purpose of the vision of the wounds as evoking in us a similar joyous countenance. She even uses the very same words; the Lord has 'a glad cheer' and so the vision is to make us 'glad and merry'. Though we are still in the realm of passion meditation, Julian brings a sense of resurrection joy and gladness right into the heart of the passion and its pain.

Just like the Man of Sorrows, Julian's description of Christ in this opening section of chapter 24 combines into one the dichotomy of the passion and resurrection. In this way, her tenth vision draws the reader to recall the words Jesus speaks to Thomas at the end of John 20: 'Blessed are those who have not seen and yet have believed', as the English translation of the Latin Vulgate states. The tenth revelation opens with a vision of reassurance for the blessed as Julian develops Jesus' words to Thomas to reach out and put his hand in Jesus' wounded side.

Entering Christ's wound

Like many devotional writers of her time, Julian imaginatively takes this invitation to reach out and touch the wounds of the resurrected Christ one stage further. Julian enters right into the wound, like going into a cavern of flesh, with Jesus as her guide. This same devotional invitation can also be found in the image from the French book of hours. As if to help us contemplate the wounds of Christ more deeply, the left-hand side of the image is totally dominated by a proportionately life-size representation of the wound in his side. The French words that encircle the life-size wound read: '*Ci est la mesure de la plaie du coste notre seigneur qui pour nous soffrist mort en la crois*' ('This is the measure of the cost of the wound of our Lord who for us suffers death on the cross').

We cannot know how much Julian was aware of the 13th century *Ancrene Wisse*, but there is a strong likelihood that she knew of the conventional understanding of Christ's wounds as a place for the sinner to find refuge, and was also aware of the strong images it left in the imagination. In the chapter on temptations, the author of *Ancrene Wisse* advises the anchoress that at such times she must:

> Flee into his wounds. He loved us so much who allowed such holes to be made in him for us to hide in. Creep into them with your thought – are they not entirely open? – and bloody your heart with his precious blood.
>
> *Ancrene Wisse*, Part IV

Julian's visionary probing within the wounds of Christ leads not so much to small gaps and spaces, like the clefts of rock mentioned in Song of Songs 2:14, on which the image in the *Ancrene Wisse* is based, but rather to a cavernous place where all those who shall be saved can find rest and peace. Deep within the humanity of Christ we find a new Eden, a recovery of what was lost through the fall. While the place is large enough for all humanity, Julian is orthodox in her vision and states that this place is for all Christians who shall be saved – this place, therefore, is the church. Here we begin to see the tension between Julian's revelation and the teaching of 'holy church' which will erupt in her thirteenth showing. In that showing Jesus tells her that 'all shall be well', but how does this square with the church's teaching on damnation?

We may think this is rather a leap of the imagination, from the garden of Eden to the barn of the church, but it is one we are invited to make. Immediately following this image, Christ brings to Julian's mind 'his dear worthy blood and precious water which he let pour out for love', a reference to the sacraments of the Eucharist and baptism. Of course, on one level this is a direct reference to John 19:34, where we find the account of bystanders seeing blood and water flowing from the wound made by the spear piercing Jesus' side after he had died. But this event soon came to be understood on another level as representing the birth of Lady Ecclesia, the church who, in late iconography, was also depicted as catching the saving drops in her chalice, in order to dispense them in the form of the sacrament of the Eucharist and baptism. Salvation becomes tangible and real in the sacrament of the church for it is here that the believer is deeply connected and sustained through the life-giving water and blood of Christ. Julian therefore roots her vision within 'holy church'. It is here in the barn of Christ that reassurance of sins forgiven and of the fact that all shall be well is found.

The cloven heart

In the long version of *Revelations of Divine Love* there is a sense that Julian did not so much see the blood and water pouring out of Christ's open wound as nourishment for the blessed believer in visionary terms, but rather that this was brought to her mind at this time. As Julian contemplates her vision of salvation, she is responding to it in meditative ways, which are similar to that of unpeeling the iconographic layers of the devotional image of the Man of Sorrows, which we find in many books of hours at this time. 'The sweet beholding' Julian sees is the heart of Jesus cloven in two.

Whereas devotion to the sacred heart today is widespread and has been influenced and formed by the visionaries of the 16th through to the 19th centuries, in the 14th century the devotion was still bound up with that of the wounds of Christ. As Julian reflects here, the wound in Christ's side breaks open and reveals the love, or heart, of Christ, from which the healing sacrament of water and blood pours, rather than as a devotional focus in itself. As James of Milan expresses beautifully in his *Stimulus Amoris*: 'If you meditate well on his passion and enter far within his side, you will soon come to his heart.' Perhaps what is important for Julian is that this heart is broken, 'cloven in two' as if the love of Christ could not be fully known or revealed until he had been strung up on the cross, to suffer and be rejected; until his heart had been broken on the cross.

At this point a comparison between Julian's long and short versions of her text becomes valuable. Much of the tenth revelation is absent from the short text, and instead is condensed into a brief paragraph:

> Full merrily and gladly our lord looked into his side and beheld and said, 'Lo how I love you', as if he had said, 'My child, if you cannot look in my godhead see here how I let open my side and my heart be cloven in two and let out blood and water all that was therein. And this delights me, and so will I that it also does you.' This was shown by our lord to me to make us glad and merry.

We find here the same cloven heart, blood and water, the same merry and glad countenance of the Lord, but the word 'we' is missing. We, like Julian, stand outside the body of Christ, and it is the Lord who looks into his side and opens his wound to let the healing, reconciling waters flow out. There's no messy groping into his flesh or place for us to hide. We are not involved in this vision.

The reason for this difference can be found in those vital words Jesus says: 'if you cannot look in my godhead, then contemplate my humanity.' In the short text, the Godhead is seen as being beyond us and hidden within the humanity of Christ. Similarly, in chapter 19 of the long text Julian had chosen to see heaven as 'the blessed humanity of Christ', having decided that she does not want to contemplate the Father. Rather, amid all the visions of suffering,

Julian chooses Jesus on the cross as her heaven. Now, as we have moved into the visions of salvation, something has changed, and she looks deep within the wounds of Christ and through his broken heart to see the Godhead.

It is as if we were back at the first revelation, when Julian says the most remarkable things about the cross. She sees the blood trickling down Jesus' face, as the crown of thorns is forced on to his head, but suddenly, instead of an attitude of sorrow and compassion, her heart is filled with joy. From earth to heaven in one glorious leap, perhaps, but if read in light of the tenth revelation, it is more a movement into the humanity of Christ which encloses and contains the Godhead or heaven within. In chapter 4 Julian stated that in all her revelations where Jesus appears, the blessed Trinity is understood to be present; she may not have seen it at first, but she did feel it. Now in this tenth revelation she sees it as well as feels it, for the blessed Godhead stirs her soul to understand the endless love that is without beginning and is and shall be forever, contained within the heart of Christ.

This comes as close to an ecstatic mystical experience as we can find in Julian. How different are those words 'Lo how I love you' in the long text from the ones in the short. They say exactly the same, but now they are filled with an outpouring of love which draws the reader into her visionary encounter with emotional intensity and joy:

'My darling, look and see your Lord, that is your maker and your endless joy. See what delight and bliss I have in your salvation, and for my love enjoy it with me now.' And also for more understanding this blessed word was said, 'Look and see that I loved you so much before I died for you, that I was willing to die for you; and now I have died for you and willingly suffered what I could. And now all my bitter pain and all my hard labour is turned into endless joy and bliss for me and for you. How should it now be that you should pray to me for anything that pleased me that I would not very gladly grant you? For my delight is your holiness and your endless joy and bliss with me.'

In comparison to the short text, which seems simply to report Jesus' words, here in the long text Julian wants us to feel it for ourselves through her writing. Her construction of this chapter has led up to this ecstatic moment in her writing, enabling us to feel and 'see' that revelation of divine love she experiences. But Julian doesn't leave it there; like a catch of breath, she holds the moment in suspension as she interprets and expands these simple words into a whole soliloquy of love. It feels intensely personal, between Julian and her Lord, but somehow, she has widened the space of encounter to include us. We are dwelling in that 'fair delightful place' deep within the wounds of Christ and contemplating for ourselves our relationship with the Godhead through the person of Jesus. Christ speaks to us, and indeed we too are caught up in his countenance of joy and gladness, so that we cannot but reflect it in ourselves.

After this rollercoaster ride in perspective, it is worth pausing to reflect on how Julian's text has managed to capture the disorientating and overwhelming sense of her visionary encounter. She has been able to express this perfectly in the way her writing has shifted through various forms of seeing, knowing and understanding. Ideas that have been brought to mind overlay the showing and then move to understanding, which undergirds the text. So, we have moved through a mixture of shades of expression that bring us through a prism of colours to the white light of encounter and where the countenance of the Lord, through her writing, is able to be reflected in us. Through her words we know and feel the joy of salvation and the deep assurance of sins forgiven.

———— *Going deeper* ————

Before you read Julian's words ask God to speak to you through them.

> Look and see that I loved you so much before I died for you, that I was willing to die for you; and now I have died for you and willingly suffered what I could. And now all my bitter pain and all my hard labour is turned into endless joy and bliss for me and for you.

As you slowly reread Julian's words, allow your imagination to hear Jesus speaking through Julian's writing.

What word or insight does he have for you today?

Reflect for a moment on where your thoughts were led, what spoke to you and why?

Not trying to silence your inner thoughts and feelings, let them float by like the flowing water of a stream and allow your attention to go deeper into silence for as little or as long as you wish.

What will you take away with you from this time of meditation?

Questions to ponder or discuss

- When and where have you known the closeness with Christ?
- How do you relate to Julian's depiction of the wound of Christ?
- What does the word 'salvation' mean to you?
- How would you describe the saving love of Christ to another?
- In what ways could you reveal Christ's redeeming presence in your life today?

Words for the journey

Soul of Christ, sanctify me.
Body of Christ, save me.
Blood of Christ, inebriate me.
Water from the side of Christ, wash me.
Passion of Christ, strengthen me.
O Good Jesus, hear me.
Within your wounds hide me.
Permit me not to be separated from you.
Anima Christi

THE ELEVENTH REVELATION

– 4 –

HIS DEAREST MOTHER

This ecstatic stage in our journey continues as the following showing takes us from the wound in Christ's side to the place of Mary at the foot of the cross. The sorrowing mother of Jesus is seen as an icon of contemplative devotion and love of Jesus but also as the exemplum of the love and joy Christ has in us. Like Mary, our experience may be one of sorrow and suffering, but the reality is that we are loved and kept by Christ, through whom all things are well.

In the eleventh showing of Julian's *Revelations of Divine Love* the scene has hardly changed, but Julian's focus has shifted from Christ's wounds to the person of Mary:

> And with this same countenance of mirth and joy our good Lord looked down on the right side and brought to my mind where our lady stood in the time of his passion; and said, 'Would you like to see her?'

As we begin this second section in Julian's visions of salvation it seems that we have moved seamlessly from one chapter to another, from one revelation to another. It is as if we are watching one long scene in a film without any cuts. The focus is exactly the same as that of the tenth revelation. We are still arrested by the countenance of Christ, which is full of joy and mirth, but this time as we follow his gaze, we are taken down his right side.

The Lord brings to Julian's mind the person who stood at the foot of the cross during Christ's suffering, his mother Mary. Once again the showing begins with reminiscences of the passion in the agony of Mary.

'Woman, here is your son'

In the scriptural account of the passion, it is only John who gives a clear record that Mary the mother of Jesus was at the foot of his cross when her son died. The synoptic gospels mention the group of women who were involved in Jesus' ministry as being present at the crucifixion, but it is disputed whether they included Mary. We cannot be sure that 'Mary, the mother of James and Joseph' (Matthew 27:56) or 'Mary the mother of James the younger and of Joseph [as per NIV]' (Mark 15:40), refer to Mary the mother of Jesus. It seems unlikely. It is therefore only through John's account that we can be certain that Mary was present at the foot of the cross:

> Near the cross of Jesus stood his mother, his mother's sister, Mary the wife of Clopas, and Mary Magdalene. When Jesus saw his mother there, and the disciple whom he loved standing near by, he said to her, 'Woman, here is your son,' and to the disciple, 'Here is your mother.' From that time on, this disciple took her into his home.
> JOHN 19:25–27

This reference may be brief but, as many Good Friday addresses will attest, there is much to ponder from these words when we liturgically place ourselves at the foot of the cross each Holy Week.

Central to the biblical passage is the importance of relationship. Jesus was Mary's eldest child, and in first-century Palestine this fact would have carried certain responsibilities, as it still does today. On a practical level, Jesus' tender words transfer the responsibility of care for his mother to that of the beloved disciple. On a spiritual level, through his words, Jesus extends the familial relationship that he had with his mother to that of John, the disciple whom Jesus loved. Now she is to be the mother of John as she was to Jesus, and he is to act as her eldest son. In this way, Jesus himself puts into practice his words recounted in Matthew 12, where he responds to those who tell him that his mother and brothers are waiting and wanting to speak to him:

> He replied to him, 'Who is my mother, and who are my brothers?' Pointing to his disciples, he said, 'Here are my mother and my brothers. For whoever does the will of my Father in heaven is my brother and sister and mother.'
> MATTHEW 12:48–50

At the foot of the cross Jesus' words to Mary and John place all of us who would follow Christ into a special relationship not only with his mother Mary, but also with each other and ultimately with him, which is based upon familial ties. It is these scriptural passages which undergird Julian's eleventh showing.

Devotion to Mary, the mother of God

Devotion to the person of Mary during the 14th century was profound and prevalent. One example of this devotion, and the power of its expression in illumination, can be seen in the exquisite Sherborne missal. This public manuscript of the Mass was commissioned by Robert Bruyning, who was abbot of the Benedictine abbey of St Mary's in Sherborne from 1385–1415, so we can date it to around the time that Julian was alive. The missal was an important book for all medieval churches and monastic houses to own, as it contained the prayers, text and calendar required for celebrating the Eucharist, as it does today. Being such an important public book, it was therefore highly valued and, if the church or foundation was rich enough, was often elaborately illuminated, making it a treasure of the community. Therefore, it is unsurprising that the creation and use of the manuscript became an act of devotion in itself. The Sherborne missal was not only a working book but also a piece of devotional art through which the community was invited to meditate and pray.

The page which precedes the climax of the Mass, the Eucharistic prayer, is dominated by an image of the crucifixion (see Plate 4). Just as Julian sees in her revelation, Christ is shown looking down to his right with eyes that are barely open due to the agony he is in. There is no countenance of gladness in Christ's face. Rather this is a depiction of the Man of Sorrows who engenders meditation on his suffering on the cross. The scene is populated by numerous people seemingly jostling for the attention of the person looking at this image. One of them, in a rather nonchalant manner, sticks his lance into Christ's side and from it pours the blood and water of the Eucharist.

While Christ is central to this image, as one would expect in an illumination that reflects the sacrifice of the Eucharist, he does not dominate the composition of the piece. Instead, it is Mary, wrapped in azure blue swooning at the foot of the cross, who dominates. She is the one to whom the artist wanted our eye to be drawn and to be held by. The reason for this may have been as a result of the abbey being dedicated to Mary. But this composition of the passion scene also expressed the seminal aspect of devotion to Mary in the late 14th century, which was to the *Stabat Mater* or Sorrowing Mother.

Stabat Mater Dolorosa

Since the time of St Anselm, a strong tradition had grown up around the brief, yet highly poignant, scriptural passage in John's gospel. It encouraged the devout to enter deeply into an imaginative engagement with the scene that placed them at the foot of the cross along with Mary. At the heart of this devotion was the image of the sorrowing mother, which is encapsulated in the 13th-century Franciscan hymn called the *Stabat Mater Dolorosa*. The hymn begins by describing Mary at the scene of the passion beholding her son in abject sorrow and agony, but the focus quickly shifts to us and how we respond to her suffering. In the language of prayer, we are invited to make this sorrowing our own, as the hymn seeks to evoke in us the same love for Christ as Mary had. It was this popular devotional desire that Julian sought as a young girl when she asked to be given the gift of 'mind of his passion'.

Alongside the liturgical and devotional emphasis on the *Stabat Mater* in prayer and prose, we cannot underestimate the visual impact that the figure of the weeping Mary, along with that of John, had on those who entered their local parish church. Statues of sadness which rose high into the apex of the chancel, suspended as they were above the rood screen, often dominated the interior of medieval churches. Immediately, the onlooker would not only have been reminded of the passion and the faithful vigil of Mary and John with the suffering Christ, but also be physically placed at the foot of the cross along with them.

This familiar and prevailing motif also adorned the walls and was refracted in light through stained glass windows, as well as filling the pages of illuminated manuscripts, such as gospels, missals and the books of hours or personal prayer books. In both public worship and private prayer, the image of Mary drew the devout into ever deeper and more profound meditation on the love of Christ through her sufferings and sorrow. From dignified grief to collapsed agony, Mary epitomised the human response to the suffering of Christ on the cross. She was the icon of perfect love for him, which the devout of the medieval world sought to emulate through engagement with her at the foot of the cross.

While the gospel account of this moment in Mary's life is brief, through the medieval tradition of lyrics and passion meditations, the imagination was encouraged to explore and embellish not only Jesus' last words to his mother but also how she might have felt at seeing her son die and what she could have said in those final agonising moments. These could vary greatly in form from that of a complaint, in which Mary addresses the reader in the style of a monologue of agony, to conversation with her son.

A good example of the former is found in the preaching book of the Franciscan John Grimestone, which was written in 1372 and probably originates from south-west Norfolk. The silent scriptural figure of Mary is given a voice in this lyric as the poet imagines what she might have said as she watched her son suffer. In this medieval affective tradition of spirituality, such poems sought not only to imaginatively take us back to the moments of the passion but also bring Mary's profound sorrows into the present so that those who read these words could intimately relate to her through the devotional language and tropes of the 14th-century world. Her words are heartrending and full of pleading to the bystanders. As such they bring forth in the reader a deep sense of compassion and shared agony for the mother who must bear such suffering. The lyric calls forth compassion for her sorrows but also reflects to the reader how they are to respond with similar compassion and devotion to the suffering of Christ.

'Would you like to see her?'

The normative response which the devout were encouraged to feel in response to Mary at the foot of the cross was that of compassion and sorrow. But the countenance of the Lord teaches Julian to look on this scene very differently. As with the tenth showing, we are also to behold this eleventh vision not with sorrow but with joy and praise. In a moving and tender section of her text, Christ reveals to Julian a vision of his mother Mary, who, in his love for her, reflects back to us the hidden reality of our relationship with Christ and how we can fully respond to his love.

And in the sweet word, it was as if he said: 'I well know that you would like to see my blessed mother, for after myself she is the highest joy that I might show you, and the highest delight and honour to me; and most she is to be seen of my blessed creatures.' And for the exalted, marvellous and singular love that he has to this sweet maiden, his blessed mother, our lady Saint Mary, he showed her highly rejoicing, which is the meaning of these sweet words, as if he had said: 'Would you like to see how I love her, so that you may rejoice with me in the love that I have for her and she for me?' And also, to more understand this sweet word our lord God speaks to all mankind that shall be saved as if it were all to one person, as if he said: 'Would you like to see in her how you are loved? For love of you I made her so exalted, so noble and of such worth; and this delights me, and I want it to delight you.'

The eleventh showing shifts from the idea of a vision of the sorrowing Mary at the foot of the cross, which the showing initially brought to Julian's mind, to a 'ghostly' or spiritual revelation of Mary 'high and noble and glorious'. We, like Julian, have interpreted Christ's attitude of looking down his right side with the tropes and ideas of the sorrowing mother at the foot of cross. The eleventh showing is a revelation of Mary but not as Julian thinks; rather it is how much Jesus loves her.

Again, we have gone beyond the veil to see the reality of Jesus' relationship with his mother which was hidden in that time of suffering but now is revealed in all its profound intimacy. The showing becomes a lesson in love and assurance to reveal to us just how we also stand in the place and relationship of love as Mary does.

A lesson in love

The tone of the revelations at this point shifts away from the narrative and meditation tropes of the passion to the notion of visionary encounter, which is precipitated by dialogue. Up to this point, Julian has heard words spoken in her vision, either generally or in kind, but only twice has this been by Christ. Notably, in the sixth showing, where he thanks Julian for the hard labour of her youth, and then again in the ninth. It is in the latter that the locutions of Christ really begin to escalate within the revelations, until Julian is in open debate with him.

It is interesting that this shift correlates to the move from a focus on the cross to the revelations of salvation and is initiated by words of satisfaction and reparation through atonement. The barriers which prevented open encounter with God begin to collapse during the ninth showing as Christ not only asks Julian if she is well satisfied that he suffered for her but goes on to state: 'If you are satisfied, I am satisfied. It is a joy, a bliss, and endless delight to me that ever I suffered the passion for you, and if I might suffer more, I would suffer more.' Through these words Julian is taken up into heaven, where she sees a vision of the three heavens of the Trinity, an act which parallels her experience in the first revelation, where she looked at the cross of Christ and her heart was filled with joy by the Trinity.

In the following tenth revelation this mode of dialogue with Christ is continued, as he invites Julian into his cloven heart with the words: 'Lo, how I loved you.' The showing of the passion is transfigured by his words from a place of the suffering of Christ into a demonstration of his love, as he opens his wounds from which run the water and blood of the Eucharist. Now, in the eleventh showing, Christ's question of 'Would you like to see her?' calls for a response from Julian, which will initiate a vision in its own right. Her answer of 'Yes' moves her and us beyond the veil of human agony and death of the passion to the vision of salvation that it contains, epitomised in the glory of Mary. But before we arrive at this moment of revelation, Julian goes back again and again to add in the steps she took in her understanding to get to the deeper significance of Christ's words.

Looking at the short text alongside that of the long, one could be forgiven for feeling that Julian has overcomplicated a simple revelation with her layers of interpretation. But in a way these layers are a lesson which teaches us just how much Mary is loved by Christ, but also how much he loves us in turn. We can see this if we look at each of the steps along the way. These steps are each introduced with the phrase 'as if he said' and are followed by Julian's subsequent interpretation, which is presented still as being the words of Christ.

The first refers to the special status that Mary holds to Jesus as his mother:

> I well know that you would like to see my blessed mother, for after myself she is the highest joy that I might show you, and the highest delight and honour to me; and most she is to be seen of my blessed creatures.

It reflects the tenderness between them, that is often beautifully captured in images of the mother and child of that period, such as the stained-glass Madonna and Child found in the east window of the church at Eaton Bishop in Herefordshire (see Plate 5). Dating from 1320 to 1340 this beautiful Gothic design shows an exquisite Mary crowned as queen of heaven, looking into the eyes of her child, who lovingly touches her face in a gesture that captures a very familiar intimacy between a child and his mother. It is this same intimacy that Julian sees underlying the invitation from Christ to see his mother, for above all creatures she is most precious and beloved by him.

In the next layer of significance, it is this contemplation of love that becomes explicit as Julian places a declaration of love into the words of Jesus: 'Would you like to see how I love her, so that you may rejoice with me in the love that I have for her and she for me?' As Julian contemplates the simple words of Christ which invite her to see his mother, she begins to perceive that they are more than just about a showing but are also an invitation to take part in the intimate relationship of love between Mary and Jesus. Like a child who is proud of his mother, Christ wants us to share in his joy and love for her. He offers to make us one of his family and incorporate us into that circle of intimate love. The exclusiveness of the shared look between the stained-glass Madonna and Child is transformed for Julian into an inclusiveness through her meditation on his simple words of invitation.

The loving gaze of the Madonna and Child has shifted in its focus away from the singular love between Christ and Mary, who epitomises the perfect and fullest response to that love, to look on us. Julian realises that, in these simple words of invitation, 'Would you like to see her', Jesus is giving a lesson in love through the person of Mary. Mary is the icon or forerunner of the relationship of love with Christ which, as a result of the atonement, we are all invited into. In his question Jesus calls us to stand in the place of Mary and, like her, to respond to that invitation to intimacy with the word 'Yes'. It is not insignificant that Julian's reply to Christ's words echoes that of the annunciation. Just as Mary entered into a deep spiritual and physical relationship with God through saying 'Yes' to the angel Gabriel, so Julian's response of 'Yes' opens up a new showing that reveals a spiritual sight of Mary glorified.

Visions of Mary

Numerous visionaries before her, not least Bridget of Sweden and Elizabeth of Hungary as well as Margery Kempe in King's Lynn, gave accounts of the visions and conversations they had had with Mary, even to the extent of helping Mary bath baby Jesus. However, Julian realised that she was not going to be given such a bodily vision, though she may have desired it. Instead, she received a spiritual vision of Mary's blessed soul, her truth, wisdom and love, so that Julian 'may learn to know myself and reverently fear my God'. Julian's visions of Mary were to enable her and us to learn and understand what the fullest and most perfect response to Christ's love is. Mary reveals this response, rather than focusing on the life and person of herself. For it was Mary who responded absolutely to the love of Christ, so much so that they were united in love.

Just as the crowning of Mary was seen as the pinnacle of her life, so Christ's words to Julian of delight and joy in many ways encapsulate this culmination of Julian's visions about Mary throughout her revelations. These have shown Mary as a young girl at the annunciation, sorrowing at the foot of the cross and finally high and noble as the queen of heaven. In each case Mary's response to Christ's love is epitomised by her attitude, which Julian describes as 'reverent dread'. Throughout Julian's text, Mary is the icon of loving devotion to Christ, the elegant, deeply respectful and humble response to God which she showed in her words to the angel at the rnnunciation. She is also the exemplum who shows us how we are to love and how much we are loved, however it may feel to the opposite in our ordinary lives.

Going deeper

Spend some time with Christ's words to Julian:

> And also, to more understand this sweet word our lord God speaks to all mankind that shall be saved as if it were all to one person, as if he said: 'Would you like to see in her how you are loved? For love of you I made her so exalted, so noble and of such worth; and this delights me, and I want it to delight you.'

Reflect on a time when God felt very close to you. What was it that enabled you to feel close to God?

Reflect on a time when God felt distant. What was it that prevented you from knowing and feeling God's presence?

What are the needs and secret longings of your heart that you would like to lay before Jesus?

Allow your inner thoughts and feelings to float away like clouds across the moon and rest in the loving presence of your Beloved in silence and peace.

What will you take away with you from this time of meditation?

Questions to ponder or discuss

- How does this extract make you feel?
- How is Mary an icon for the perfect response to God's love?
- What do you understand by the term 'reverend dread'?
- In what ways have you responded to Christ's call?
- How could you encourage someone in their journey of faith this week?

Words for the journey

My soul doth magnify the Lord. And my spirit hath rejoiced in God my Saviour. For he hath regarded the low estate of his handmaiden: for, behold, from henceforth all generations shall call me blessed. For he that is mighty hath done to me great things; and holy is his name.

LUKE 1:46–49 (KJV)

*

THE TWELFTH REVELATION

– 5 –

CHRIST OUR SAVIOUR

Our journey reaches the mountain top and takes us above the clouds and beyond the mist to a mystical vision of the person of Jesus Christ, who he is and how much we are held and loved by him. It is an experience which we may never have in this life, but Julian reaches to the edge of the capacity of language in her attempt to describe this encounter for us. It is the ultimate statement that through the passion and resurrection of Jesus Christ we do not need to live by fear anymore but by the hidden reality of faith which believes that all is well.

After this our lord showed himself more glorified, as it seemed to my sight, than I had seen him before, wherein I learned that our soul shall never have rest until it comes to know his that is the fullness of joy, homely and courteous bliss and true life. Our Lord Jesus oftentimes said: 'I it am, I it am: I it am that is highest; I it am that you love; I it am that you like; I it am that you serve; I it am that you long for; I it am that you desire; I it am that is your meaning; I it am that is all; I it am that "holy church" preaches and teaches; I it am that showed me here to you.'

The number of the words surpassed my wit and all my understanding and all my might, for they are the most exalted, as it seems to me; for what therein is comprehended – I cannot tell; but the joy that I saw in the showing surpasses all that the heart may wish and the soul may desire; and therefore the words cannot be explained here but everyone after the grace that God has given him may receive our lords meaning in their understanding and loving.

Until now Julian has taken us on the journey of her visionary experience, leading us into the humanity of Christ through his wounds to an encounter of love. Mary has then been modelled to us as the ultimate receptor and response of Christ's love, and we have come to share in the delight Christ has in her and realised that in her we see how much we are loved. Now the image of Mary fades and instead we are called deeper and higher on our spiritual path, being pulled by the forces of love, to contemplate Christ himself. We leave the cross far away, as the clouds of sorrow depart and Christ is revealed in all his glory.

Unlike the previous two revelations, which seemed to meld into each other and were differentiated only by their shift of focus within one scene of contemplation, the twelfth revelation is quite separate. Julian moves us in a clear and definite way. Perhaps this was how she experienced her twelfth revelation. It came to her not as an unfolding aspect of an entire revelatory experience, but rather as a breaking in, a spontaneous act of pure gift. Even if the chapter heading and summary had not been in the text, we would still hear and feel in her words that something has changed. We have moved into a different realm, of which the meditation on Christ's wounds and the contemplation of Mary were but staging posts to a higher contemplation of God in the person of Jesus Christ.

In his brief guide to the contemplative life, the author of *The Cloud of Unknowing* tells us that while it is good to meditate on the kindness of the Lord, the kindness of our lady or even on the joys in heaven, these need to be left behind under a cloud of forgetting in order to contemplate and praise the being of God in the cloud of unknowing. There is a sense that this is what is going on here as we move into chapter 26. Julian has been contemplating aspects of faith which have their expression and imagery deep within the devotional culture of her age. These are now left behind under a cloud of forgetting as she receives a more glorious revelation of Christ as Saviour.

For both Julian and the *Cloud* author a seminal aspect of this experience is the extent to which the soul is drawn, pulled towards God by the magnetic forces of desire within the soul. Whether this be purely apophatic or in darkness, as the *Cloud* author expresses it, or whether it be cataphatic or in light, as through the person of Christ in Julian's vision, both take us beyond the veil to knowing God in and for himself alone. St Augustine's famous words from his *Confessions* resonated as much with the contemplative of 14th century as they do today: 'You have made us for yourself, and our hearts are restless till they find their rest in you.' Julian not only echoes these words but, like many devotional authors who have deeply experienced what St Augustine referred to, she also brings her own understanding and expression to it.

Embodying scripture and tradition

It is very probable that Julian did not have the depth or breadth of education that most of us are fortunate enough to enjoy today. Schools for nuns or tutors for girls would have given a simple and basic education at best, which consisted mainly of basic reading and perhaps writing, if they were lucky. Instead, women like Julian would have primarily learned through conversation in the rich aural world of the late 14th century, where ideas were debated and discussed, argued over and mused upon. Julian would not have been separated from this, even in her anchorhold. She may not have been learned in the sense of knowing Latin or having studied in the scholastic schools, but she was highly educated in her knowledge of scripture, theology and philosophy, for the 14th-century world turned upon its understanding of the universe through faith.

In our postmodern world it can be difficult for us to imagine ourselves back in the faith-based world of the medieval period, where everything from cradle to grave was shaped and defined by the story of salvation. Within her writings we see how Julian lived and breathed the stories of scripture and the theological knowledge of her day. Her text resounds with references and allusions which can be traced back to numerous religious writers and theological thinkers, let alone the Bible. In fact, it is often hard to discern where Julian speaks and where she verbalises the ideas and thinking of her day.

It was second nature for Julian to speak the language of faith and spirituality as if it were her own. Hence at the beginning of chapter 26 we are not given a quotation or even an allusion to Augustine, let alone a footnote and reference to the page and line of the *Confessions*, which cite his perceptive insight into the nature of God and the yearning we have for him in the human heart. In good plagiaristic terms, Julian simply makes his truth her own, as his words verbalise a universal truth which is known to all who seek God. Instead, Julian takes the sense of his words to express her own understanding of what he tries to verbalise about the call of God:

> Wherein I learned that our soul shall never have rest till it comes to him knowing that he is the fullness of joy, homely and courteously blissful and our very life.

In this sentence there are two words which spring off the page for anyone who knows the writings of Julian: homely and courteous. They mean very different things, but Julian brings them together here to express the nature of God as it was revealed to her in May 1373.

Humble courtesy

This is one of several times that Julian uses 'homely', each time its meaning shifts slightly as she moulds it in her hands to express a deepening awareness of the nature of our relationship with God. It is in chapter 5 that Julian really begins to unpack the meaning of the state of *homlyhede*, the insight into our intimate relationship with God that she gained from her first revelation of the crowning of thorns. Here the term expresses the humility of Christ on the cross in terms of a domestic image of clothing, in order to convey the extent to which God's love humbly enters everyday human life, enclose us and be everything that is good for us.

Now in chapter 26 we find this word being used once again with that same idea of the humility of God as found in chapters 4 and 5. But here it is also paired with the language of courtly behaviour, lest we forget that this is the high king of heaven who draws us to partake in his glory as he does in our humanity. In this pairing of the language of humility and courtly behaviour to describe what knowing the fullness of God is like, Julian once more brings in the notion of reverent dread, which we saw Mary epitomising in the last revelation. There Mary was presented to us as the icon and exemplar of the humble marvelling at the condescension of God to be born of her a simple creature. It was this deep attitude of reverent dread, her humility and self-emptying, that enabled God in turn to self-empty, take on the form of a slave and be born in human likeness. Because of this gracious act of humility by Mary, Christ in turn presents her to us as the high queen of heaven in a gesture of sublime courtesy to her. Revealing that the end of all our yearning and searching is to know and come to this attitude of reverent dread as revealed and exemplified by Mary.

I am who I am

Jesus now speaks again as he has done throughout these three revelations, but the manner of his words has changed. They have taken on a rhetorical edge and are climatic in the way they build one upon another in the repetition of 'I it am'. In the Middle English this has a powerful triple syllable resonance, holding within each statement the Trinitarian truth, which is present wherever Jesus is seen in Julian's revelations:

I it am, I it am: I it am that is highest; I it am that you love; I it am that you like; I it am that you serve; I it am that you long for; I it am that you desire; I it am that is your meaning; I it am that is all; I it am that 'holy church' preaches and teaches; I it am that showed me here to you.

The base text on which Julian's vision springs is Exodus 3:13–15, where Moses addresses God in the burning bush and asks what name he is to use to the Israelites to say who has sent him. In reply, Yahweh states, 'I am who I am' and then goes on to instruct Moses to say that 'I am has sent me to you.' As if to clarify still further, God then gives a relational name: '"Yahweh, the God of your ancestors, the God of Abraham, the God of Isaac, and the God of Jacob, has sent me to you": This is my name forever and this my title for all generations' (v. 15, NRSV). Alongside the name of God from the Hebrew Bible, Julian's vision also resonates with the 'I am' sayings of John's gospel, where Jesus uses the phrase to describe attributes about himself. Julian's showing thereby holds together both the revelation of the name of Yahweh in the Old Testament and the revelation of who Jesus Christ is in the New Testament.

The name of Jesus

During the 14th century Norwich became a centre for devotion to the name of Jesus, which was widely popularised through the writings of the early 14th-century German Dominican friar Henry Suso. The close relationship Norwich enjoyed with the Low Countries through commerce meant that there was a free flow of ideas and new trends from abroad. S new liturgical feast was brought in to honour the Holy Name and numerous devotional writers were attracted to this cult and the awesome power and healing properties which invocation to the name of Jesus contained. From the 14th century onwards, there was increasing use of the monogram IHS, the first three letters of Jesus in Greek ΙΗΣΟΥΣ, to represent the name of Jesus. For example, it was displayed along with the instruments of the passion surrounding the frame of the 14th-century Despenser retablo in Norwich Cathedral (see Plate 6). Such was the power of the name of Jesus.

The notion that Jesus' name could somehow hold power within itself has its roots in scripture. Both Acts 16:18 and Mark 9:38–39 tell of individuals who called on the name of Jesus to receive particular protection from evil. The first is Paul, who orders a spirit of divination to come out of a slave girl in the name of Jesus. Moreover, Jesus himself tells his disciples that no one who does a deed of power in his name will be able to speak evil of him. This devotion took on new meaning and significance especially during the time of the plague. Contemporaneous writers to Julian, such as Richard Rolle and Walter Hilton, had a deep devotion to the name of Jesus and refer to the protective power of Christ's name in their works. For example, in *The Form of Perfect Living and Other Prose Treatises* (Good Press, 2019), Richard Rolle writes:

> If you think on the name of Jesus continually, and hold it stably, it purges your sin and kindles your heart, it purifies your soul, it removes anger, it does away slowness, it wounds you with love, fulfils you in charity, chases away the devil and puts out dread, it opens heaven and makes a contemplative.

Similarly, for Walter Hilton in his *Scale of Perfection,* the name of Jesus also holds this meaning of giving health and healing and, like Rolle, he also expresses the more ecstatic element to the devotion to the name of Jesus which is found in Philippians 2:9–11:

> Therefore God exalted him to the highest place and gave him the name that is above every name, that at the name of Jesus every knee should bow, in heaven and on earth and under the earth, and every tongue acknowledge that Jesus Christ is Lord, to the glory of God the Father.
> PHILIPPIANS 2:9–11

Here we find a hymn to the glorious name of Jesus, and it is this sense which we find in Julian's revelation. While the sense of healing and protection may be implied to the medieval audience, Jesus' words to Julian are not so much an invocation by a sinner needing to be healed with the protective power of a salve, but more the disclosure of his nature, as we find in Exodus.

Julian's vision is extraordinary in its power and expression. It is as if the heaping up of words upon words, which repeat themselves in a standard formula, are a series of invocations to the name of Jesus. The only difference is that these words are not calling for aid, but expounding in short bullet-like phrases who Jesus is and what he means to us. Only the first two carry that Exodus sense of I am who I am, the rest are all relational and build one upon another: it is I who am highest, I you love, I you delight in, I whom you serve, I that you long for, I you desire, I am your purpose, I am your all. In a strange way Jesus is reversing the words of wooing we would expect. What we would expect is for the lover to say to his beloved, 'It is you who is highest, you I love, you I delight in, you whom I serve' and so on in a mode of courtly adoration, but that's not what we have here. Instead, Jesus is much more persuasive, begging even, to tell his beloved what he means to her, as if she has got it all wrong and been lured off by false suitors and fake love.

The lover-knight

In the 13th-century guide for anchoresses, the *Ancrene Wisse*, we find such a passage where Christ woos the soul. Following on from a wonderful exemplar, which describes the soul as a lady who is surrounded by her enemies, her lands ruined, destitute and locked in an earthen castle, Christ comes as the lover-knight to free her and win her love. The author goes on to state that there are four main kinds of love: that between good friends, between a man and a woman, a woman for her child, and between body and soul. The love Christ has for his beloved transcends these four and surpasses them, as he says to the soul:

> Your love… is either to be wholly a gift, or it is for sale, or it is to be taken and captured by force. If it is to be a gift, where could you bestow it better than upon me? Am I not the fairest one? Am I not the richest king? Am I not the highest born? Am I not the wisest among the rich? Am I not the most courteous of men? Am I not the most generous one?
>
> *Ancrene Wisse*, Part VII

There is much here that is comparable to Julian's words: the same insistence and the same 'I am' statements. But in the *Ancrene Wisse* it is clear that these, unlike Julian's showing, are used as accusatory questions, rather than statements of disclosure. We are also clear in the *Ancrene Wisse* that it is a man talking to a woman, Christ the lover-knight to the lady of the soul, but in Julian there is none of this imagery implied. For here we are not in the world of symbolism or tropes, but rather in a place where Christ's words can and are spoken to anyone regardless of gender. Julian makes this fact explicit in the way she alters the short text and takes out a reference to contemplatives as being the ones who would receive such a vision as this. Similarly, at the end of the chapter, Julian writes that these words were not just given to her but that 'everyone, according to the grace that God gives him in understanding and loving, receive them as our Lord intended'.

So, Julian closes this chapter with a statement of openness and even mystery. For it is clear that these 'I it am' statements, which she records, were not the only ones given: 'Oftentimes our lord Jesus said.' The opening statement to the 'I it am' sayings gives us a window into how this vision revealed itself. The repetitive layering of language expresses, in literary form, a sense of the overflowing desire of Jesus to reveal who he is, peeling away the layers of blindness, until Julian's words begin to groan and creak as they try to express the inexpressible and ineffable.

Finally, Julian takes us to the edge of the ability of language to convey her experience and it collapses into: 'I cannot tell, but the joy that I saw in the showing surpassed all that heart may will and soul may desire, and therefore the words cannot be declared here.' If you ever wondered whether it was right to call Julian a mystic, then here I think is your proof. In her twelfth revelation Christ reveals himself and what he means to her, a revelation which words cannot communicate but can only be experienced. Hence Julian leaves us with this mystery: that just beyond the veil, Christ desires above all else to disclose to us that he is our all. We may never experience this for ourselves this side of eternity, but we have her words to contemplate and make our own, while we also have the person of Mary to emulate.

Going deeper

Give yourself some time to linger with Julian's twelfth vision.

> I it am, I it am: I it am that is highest; I it am that you love; I it am that you like; I it am that you serve; I it am that you long for; I it am that you desire; I it am that is your meaning; I it am that is all; I it am that 'holy church' preaches and teaches; I it am that showed me here to you.

What strikes you about Christ's words to Julian?

How do they make you feel?

What would you like to say in response to them?

Let your mind soften and gently allow your thoughts to pass into the distant scene as you come into a place of stillness and wonder.

What will you take away with you from this time of meditation?

Questions to ponder or discuss

- How do you understand the word 'love' in this revelation?
- What do you resonate with in Julian's twelfth revelation of Christ as Saviour?
- How does Julian's revelation of Christ relate to social action?
- What would you want to share with someone about this revelation?
- What value does the mystical element of our faith bring to the church?

Words for the journey

It is no longer I who live, but Christ who lives in me.

GALATIANS 2:20 (ESV)

THE THIRTEENTH REVELATION

– 6 –

ALL SHALL BE WELL

In our journey through Julian's visions of salvation we have been building up to those immortal words that are known and loved by many: 'All shall be well, all shall be well, and all manner of thing shall be well.' But what does Julian really mean by them? To answer that question, we have to return to the text and chapter 27 where they first appear in her thirteenth revelation.

> After this the Lord brought to my mind the longing that I had for him before; and I saw that nothing prevented me but sin, and so I beheld generally in us all. And methought, if sin had not been, we should all have been clean and like to our Lord as he made us; and thus, in my folly, before this time often I wondered why by the great foreseeing wisdom of God the beginning of sin was not prevented; for then, methought, all should be well. These thoughts were greatly to be forsaken but nevertheless grieving and sorrowful I had them without reason and discretion. But Jesus, who in this vision informed me all that was needful to me, answered with this word and said: 'Sin is behovable but all shall be well, and all shall be well, and all manner of thing shall be well.'

We have left the world of visionary encounter far behind and returned to earth with a bump. How different is the language, tone and structure of this chapter to the last ecstatic, speech-defying moment which closed the former. It is as if we have been on the heights of Sinai or Tabor, when the cloud of unknowing has parted as mist in the morning and we have seen Christ transfigured in light and love but only for a moment. Julian's words, unable to express what she has seen, lie crumbled before her in a heap of sodden syllables to be left in silence. Only at the end has she thrown out a lifeline to us and said that we will receive her cord of broken words as far as God gives us grace in understanding and loving. But with the conditionality of this statement the mist descends once more and the moment has gone as Julian is reminded of all that prevents us from knowing that Christ is the fullness of our joy, homely and courteous, full of bliss and our true life.

Chapter 27 opens with a small ray of light; the Lord reminds Julian of the longing that she had before. Right at the beginning of her long version of *Revelations of Divine Love*, before the sickness and the night-time sufferings, before her revelations and the days, weeks, months and years of meditating upon them, before the enclosure in the anchorhold, Julian tells us of her three childhood wishes, which were common desires among the 14th-century devout. The first was to relive the passion in her imagination. The second was to receive a bodily sickness and be purged by the mercy of God to live a noble honourable life. The third was that she may receive three wounds: the wound of contrition, the wound of kind compassion and the wound of purposeful longing. Julian tells us that she forgot about the first two desires, but the third, with its three wounds, continually stayed with her. When all is lost and hidden, Julian is reminded of her first love, her childhood desire to have the wound of longing. It cannot but be noticed that just as Christ has shown his wounds to her in the tenth revelation and invited Julian to climb into them to hide and find her peace, so she is reminded now of her own reciprocal wound of love-longing, reflecting back to Christ his longing for us.

The naming of sins

As you will probably know from your own spiritual encounters, these moments of highs and lows invariably make us more aware of what mars and prevents our ability to be close to God, which is summed up in that little word called sin. Julian doesn't really go into the details by setting out all the different sins: at this point the word is obvious for her and her 14nth-century reader. But perhaps it is not so obvious for us. During the 14th century there was a very clear system of confession and penance, where the penitent had schemes to follow to ensure that their confession was full and true. One of the most significant and influential of these schemes was set up by Robert Grosseteste, the bishop of Lincoln in the 13th century. His *Templum Dei*, believed to have been written to supplement his constitutions for the diocese of Lincoln between 1239 and 1246, combined two important elements which gave clarity and purpose to this interior examination: first, a clear schematic approach which meant that complex sins and their species could be understood and remembered, and second, setting the confessional work of the priest within a larger scheme of salvation.

In both *Templum Dei* and *Deus est* (the latter a penitential tract attributed to Grosseteste) the seven deadly sins are treated in relation to love. In *Deus est* it is in the nature of human beings to love God with all their soul, all their heart and all their mind, for we consist of a soul with three parts – vegetative, sensible and rational – and a body, made up of four 'elemental' properties or cardinal virtues. Through the powers of the soul, men and women are able to love God by practising the virtues of humility, exultation, patience, generosity, spiritual activity, abstinence and continence. However, this nature has been distorted, which leads either to excess or failure in virtue, namely vice or sin. For Grosseteste, confession is seen as dealing with this failure to practise the virtues, thereby enabling the soul to, once again, love God as it was meant to. *Templum Dei* concludes with a description of the threefold life of love, namely: meditation on God, works of mercy, and knowledge of one's own wretchedness and dignity. There was plenty of opportunity to consider and gain knowledge of one's own wretchedness. It was preached daily from the pulpit, set out in devotional texts like the *Ancrene Wisse*, dealt with by spiritual directors like Richard Rolle and Walter Hilton, depicted in plays and visualised on walls. Few so-called mystical or devotional texts were without sections which gave advice on how to handle sin. We might skate over them to get to the better bits, but they are there even in Julian.

The slade of sin

Perhaps the clearest way to express how Julian saw sin and explain what she means by the words 'nothing prevented me but sin' is to turn to chapter 51, where we find an extended example of a lord and a servant that was given to her, in addition to her revelations, to answer the question of 'How does God see sin?' Here she describes the fall in terms that resonate with Anselm's theory of atonement, but what is significant for us is what happens to the beloved servant when he rushes off to do the lord's bidding. In haste to fulfil his lord's desire, the servant trips and falls into a *slade*, as Julian calls it, which means a gutter or ditch, and is badly hurt. So wounded is the servant, in fact, that he groans and moans and wallows and writhes in the ditch and is unable to look up and see the face of his loving lord, which was very near and full of comfort. Instead, as a completely enfeebled person, he can only focus on the pain and sufferings he has to bear. And so, the servant is cut off from the lord, unaware of his loving countenance, and trapped in the mire of sin. It's a wonderfully graphic image which beautifully encapsulates not only what sin is, but what it feels like. As Paul honestly says to the fledgling church in Rome:

For I have the desire to do what is good, but I cannot carry it out. For I do not do the good I want to do, but the evil I do not want to do – this I keep on doing. Now if I do what I do not want to do, it is no longer I who do it, but it is sin living in me that does it.

ROMANS 7:18–20

For Julian this sin of the miry world, or earthiness, causes blindness and folly and often prevents us from seeing our lord as our fullness of joy and life.

You can feel the frustration in Julian's words as she moves into what can only be called argumentative mode and fires that accusation at God which many still voice today: 'Why didn't you stop sin from happening? If you had, we would have been all right and just like you created us. It's your fault and you could have prevented it, then everything would have been all right.' Of course, Julian doesn't quite say it like that, but behind her gracious, wondering words, this is exactly what she means. Her words disclose to us Julian the person fighting with her own failings just like Paul: 'I should have given up these thoughts, yet I grieved and sorrowed over this, unreasonable and without discretion.' It's from this passionate outburst that the thirteenth vision now unfolds. Once again Jesus speaks to her, as he has done throughout these showings of salvation, and picks up those final words 'all shall be well' and projects them into the future so that she may know everything that is needful for her at this time. But first of all, he has to sort out sin and show how Julian is to regard it in the full scheme of salvation.

O happy fault

Jesus begins by telling Julian that 'sin is behovable'. The word 'behovable' is an interesting Middle English term which cannot easily be translated into modern English. It generally means that something is 'befitting' or 'appropriate'. The impersonal verb 'behoved' or 'behoveth', which expresses the notion of a duty or responsibility for someone to do something, was very common. But here Julian uses it as an adjective, perhaps to pick up not only the sense that it was God's responsibility to prevent sin, but also that sin itself is suitable or necessary to creation. It has its place in the grand scheme of salvation; from creation to the incarnation and eschatological fulfilment, sin plays a necessary part.

It may well be that what lies behind this use of the word is the theological doctrine of the happy fault, which lies at the heart of the great Exsultet hymn sung at the end of the Easter vigil to mark the climax of the liturgical celebrations of Easter. Here the cantor sings:

O truly necessary sin of Adam,
destroyed completely by the death of Christ!
O happy fault
that earned for us so great, so glorious a Redeemer!

If we go to the other end of the liturgical year, you will probably recognise this theological idea of the *felix culpa* or happy fault also making an appearance in the Christmas carol that often follows the reading of the fall in the ceremony of nine lessons and carols:

Adam lay ybounden,
Bounden in a bond;
Four thousand winter
Thought he not too long.

And all was for an apple,
An apple that he took.
As clerkes finden written
In their book.

Nor had one apple taken been,
The apple taken been,
Then had never our lady
A-been heaven's queen.

Blessed be the time
That apple taken was!
Therefore we may singen
Deo gratias!

Both of these liturgical moments of the past and present still convey the medieval notion that in some way the fall was a 'happy fault' or *necessārium* or 'behovely' to the scheme of salvation.

The theologian Denys Turner has brought in another associative word to 'behovely' which is the Latin *conveniens,* from which we get the word 'convenient'. To the great medieval theologians like Anselm, Hugh of Victor, Thomas Aquinas and Bonaventure it had a slightly different sense from convenient, meaning more like 'it is fitting' or is 'just so'. In this sense sin is therefore seen as *conveniens* or 'fitting' within the grand scheme of things, namely the grand scheme of salvation. For the early 14th-century Franciscan theologian Duns Scotus, however, this grand scheme needed to be viewed backwards to be understood. Instead of placing the fall as the progenitor of God's need to act, Scotus argued that God had eternally willed the Son to be the head of a glorified creation. From this eschatological viewpoint, the fall is then seen as a necessary part of God's will for his creation, which enabled the incarnation and then the passion of Christ to not only deal with sin, but also to glorify humanity through Christ.

Julian's text resonates more widely with the medieval idea not only of the happy fault, but also that Christ's incarnation was part of God's wider plan. This can be seen if we return to chapter 51 and our poor servant who is groaning and moaning in the ditch unable to see the loving countenance of the lord. As Julian explores the meaning and symbolism of this example, she soon comes to realise that, while the servant is Adam – everyman, because of his unity with all humanity – he is also Christ who falls into the clay of this human life of flesh. The pains he experiences, while they are the pains of sin, are in fact the suffering on the cross by Christ for all that sin is and takes upon himself all the blame which it incurs and produces. The example ends with the servant standing before the throne of God wearing a crown of riches on his head, for 'we are his crown, the Father's joy, the Son's worship, the Holy Ghost's liking and endless marvellous bliss to all that be in heaven'. This is the same revelation of truth that we saw in the twelfth vision. But the example shows that while this is the truth of what Christ is and who we are, in this life we will still experience the sorrow and woe of the mire. Yet this is surpassed for the joy that is ours in Christ Jesus. Hence Jesus' words state that 'sin is behovely, but all shall be well'.

We only find these words in the long text; the short text moves straight from the statement 'sin is behovely' into a description of what sin is. For Julian sin has no substance but is only known by its effects – the pain it causes and the wounds it leaves. She does not underestimate how damaging this can be to the soul even when it leads us to find comfort in the passion of our Lord. In the long text she comes back to this statement and gives it the eschatological perspective: 'sin is behovely' but 'all shall be well'. As if to outweigh the power of sin and break it down with insistence, Julian repeats the words 'all shall be well' and then expands them to be all-inclusive: 'all manner of thing shall be well'. In this way Julian's 'should', her statement of obligation, has been transfigured into the necessity of 'shall' and the perception of God's failure of responsibility is resolved in the light of the end time.

At this point Julian interprets these words from Christ in terms of the spiritual life, as she explains in the rest of chapter 27 how sin does have a place in the scheme of salvation. Sin may be necessary in order to purge us and make us know ourselves better. It may also enable us to know the virtues of forgiveness, compassion and mercy, but in the end 'all shall be well, all shall be well, and all manner of things shall be well'. Julian also sees in the tender tone of Jesus' words that for those who are safe or saved, there is no blame for sin. Instead, she is encouraged not to be so hard on herself for her sins. In a time when private confession easily encouraged scrupulosity for sin, these words are quite radical.

Chapter 27 ends with an addition to the short text that introduces the vision of a 'high, marvellous *privite*' or secret that is hid within the heart of God. In language that resonates with imagery from the books of Daniel and Revelation, Julian reiterates that we will know why God allowed sin in the world when the seals are broken or the books of heaven are opened at the end time. Till then all is hidden in the secret will of God. This eschatological vision does not so much answer Julian's question of why God allows sin as to present a Job-like response – it is not for you to know now, but there will come a time when all will be revealed. It contains within it an implicit hope that then we shall see how all will be well and sin is indeed 'behovely'.

Universal salvation

Julian is not going to accept this response so easily, for the statement 'all shall be well, all manner of things shall be well' is inherently problematic, both for Julian and for us today. One of the problems with Jesus' words to Julian that 'all shall be well' is that it can seem to devalue and reduce the many trials of this life into a glib response of 'Don't worry, it will be all right in the end.' It can seem to be pushing away a person's legitimate suffering into an undefined future and thus does not take seriously the present troubles that so many experience. And what about all those situations when it is clear that all will not be well in the end?

There is also an inherent theological problem to Julian's revelation that 'all shall be well' in that it seems to imply the concept of *apokatastasis* or universal salvation. Put simply, this is the belief that whatever you do in life, God will make it all right in the end, that the reality of human freedom to commit sin is never powerful enough to overcome the saving will of God. You don't need to be a theologian to realise that this concept, however attractive or popular it may be, raises some serious questions. If God is going to make everything all right in the end, even my sins, then why bother trying so hard to be good? And if God is going to overturn or trump our human will, how can that human will be at all called free? And what about justice and the judgement of God? If all will be well, then there is no final judgement, the sheep and goats are equally saved, and justice is no longer meted out. Finally, and here's the rub for Julian, this vision of universal salvation goes directly against the teachings of 'holy church', not only then but also now. Today one is unlikely to be burnt at the stake for holding views of universal salvation, but with the clampdown on Lollardy in the early 15th-century, this was a distinct and present concern for Julian. Julian is not unaware of the problems these words by Jesus raise; in fact she feels them acutely, and in chapter 29 she returns to them in defiant mode: 'But at this point I stood my ground.'

How can all things be well?

Julian is not going to easily accept Christ's words that 'all shall be well', and in very expressive language she tells us how she contemplated them widely, anxiously and mournfully until she returns to address Christ. In great dread at the presumption, she demands an explanation: 'Good Lord, how might all be well for the great harm that is come by sin to your creatures?' In loving and gentle tones Christ points to the teaching of 'holy church' and the story of Christ's redemption. In the light of this great act of reparation, God gives proof that he already has and will make all things well, so his words should be understood in these terms: 'For truly I have made well the most harm of (Adam) then it is my will that you know thereby that I shall make well all that is less harm.'

Julian has been given a definitive answer in which she can trust, the incarnation and passion of Jesus Christ as taught by the church. Julian's vision and the teaching of the church have come together to reinforce one another, but still Julian is vexed and concerned by Jesus' words 'all shall be well'. This time chapter 31 opens with the indication that she has been in discussion with Jesus, pummelling him with questions and doubts about how this can be so. He answers once again, and this time his words are placed within the context of the work of the Trinity: 'I may make all things well, and I can make all things well, and I will make all things well and I shall make all this well. And you shall see yourself that all manner of things shall be well.'

Within her text you can see the way Julian logically thinks through this new development of Jesus' words. She interprets the auxiliary verbs (may, can, will) to correspond with the properties associated with the Trinity. Hence the statement 'may' is associated with the power of the Father, 'can' with the wisdom of the Son and 'will' with the love of the Holy Spirit – all combined into one Trinitarian intention of 'shall'. The Trinity is constantly working to bring peace and rest to those who are safe or shall be saved. It's not surprising that Julian soon hits the buffers in her thinking when she starts to wonder about those who are not saved and for whom all things are not well, namely the damned in hell: 'And standing all this, I thought it was impossible that all manner of thing should be well as our Lord showed.' How is she to square church teaching about damnation with Jesus' words? Julian tells us that she received no other answer about this thorny subject from the Lord except his words: 'That which is impossible to you is not impossible to me. I shall save my word in all things, and I shall make all things well.' With this clear allusion to Luke 18:26–27 ('Those who heard this asked, "Who then can be saved?" Jesus replied, "What is impossible with man is possible with God."'), Julian receives the final answer that she is going to get, in this life anyway. She never fully theologically or intellectually resolves the inherent conflict which lies between this statement of universal salvation and the teaching of the church, but instead learns to live with the tension of holding to her faith as taught to her and her vision as revealed by Christ. How they are both aspects of the truth, will ever be a mystery until the end time reveals the hidden secret of God.

Now we suffer with Christ on his cross, bearing the pains of sin; our sight is blinded and we are wounded, we cannot see with God's eyes or from his perspective of salvation. But if these four visions have shown us anything it is that we need not worry about this, for the eternal joy and presence of our Lord is still there, even if it is beyond our reality. Julian's visions have given us glimpses of hope, visions of salvation to reassure us in the midst of our suffering and pain, that Christ's words are true and indeed sin may have its place, and that the Trinity does and will indeed make all manner of things well.

——— *Going deeper* ———

Spend some time slowly reading and thinking about Julian's words:

> Sin is behovable but all shall be well, all shall be well, and all manner of things shall be well.

What do these words mean for you?

What do you find challenging about them and why?

What do you think Jesus would say to you?

Allow your time of thinking and reflection to lead you into a deeper place of prayer and love.

What will you take away with you from this time of meditation?

Questions to ponder

- What does the word 'behovable' mean to you?
- Can you think of a time when sin seemed to have a purpose?
- In what ways is there room for doubts within faith?
- How would you encourage someone to question and explore their faith?
- In what ways could Julian's words of hope be used to help and comfort someone at a difficult time in their life?

Words for the journey

He who was seated on the throne said, 'I am making everything new!'

REVELATION 21:5

THE FOURTEENTH REVELATION

− 7 −

UNITED TO GOD THROUGH PRAYER

Julian continues in her open conversation with Christ and raises the first of two pastoral issues: how are we to understand prayer and the problems of prayer in the light of his words that 'all shall be well'. The problem of dryness in prayers, and whether God actually hears us when we pray, are eternal concerns and as relevant today as they were in the 14th century. Julian's showing returns us to scripture and envisions in a new and mystical way how Christ is the ground of our prayers. She pulls back the veil of heaven and shows how Christ garners our petitionary prayers, constantly using them to good and ensuring that, though we may not see it, all may be well.

Fourteen chapters after her thirteenth revelation in chapter 27, Julian returns once more to her showings with a description of the fourteenth vision that runs from chapters 41 through to 43 of her *Revelations of Divine Love*; such was the intensity and questioning which the thirteenth showing gave rise to. But now the tone shifts once again, and this time it is from the persuasive to the pastoral in order to address a number of spiritual issues that Julian raises. The next two showings are dominated by the words of Christ as he answers Julian's questions. She is still in the discursive mode of showing, where thoughts and ideas are 'brought to the mind', rather than in a visual one, where images and ideas are amalgamated into a 'bodily' description. But Julian states that these thoughts were presented as if Christ was speaking to her directly to comfort and reveal the spiritual reality of salvation despite Julian's lived experience. In the original manuscript of the long text there is no punctuation, so it is easy for Christ's words to seem merged with Julian's thoughts and so present a seamless text that has an immediacy to it and which places us as the recipient of Christ's words of comfort and reassurance.

Many today feel that visions are very much a thing of the past and God simply does not communicate so directly with his loved ones. We live in a time, like that of the prophet Samuel, when 'the word of the Lord was rare; there were not many visions' (1 Samuel 3:1). But perhaps we are not as far from the world of Julian as we think, for there are many who would affirm that they have felt that God has spoken to them in the quiet of their hearts, much as Julian describes in this fourteenth revelation, which is focused on prayer. Throughout the centuries it is through prayer that God's lovers have most deeply responded to the love of God. It is through prayer that they have also sensed the close connection with God that directly connects us with those who have walked the path of faith before us. These are the words that Julian hears:

> And this brought our Lord suddenly to my mind and showed these words and said: 'I am the ground of your beseeching: first it is my will that you have it and since I make you to will it, and since I make you to beseech it and you do beseech it, how should it then be that you should not have your beseeching?' And thus, in the first statement, along with the three that follow, our good lord shewed me a mighty comfort, as it may be seen in the same words.

On first reading, Julian's fourteenth revelation comes across as convoluted and difficult to grasp. This was also the case for Julian, as she spends the rest of the chapter, and the two which follow, gradually unpacking their sense and significance.

Before we begin to peel away the layers of meaning, it is worth looking at the thinking and reasoning that give rise to them, for the fourteenth revelation does not appear out of the blue. Each showing is intimately connected to the others, so that Julian can speak of one revelation of love presented in a series of different showings across three days, like pearls strung out on a necklace. As the writer of a text, though, Julian can decide where she wishes to place her different showings within the flow of her writing. This ordering is not necessarily systematic, and it's clear that Julian worked and reworked her text not only to develop her thoughts, but also to adjust the position of where she placed the description of her showings, as well as the interpretation and thinking that flowed from them.

This is the case with revelation fourteen. It comes after a long section that considers the many questions that flowed from her thirteenth showing that 'all shall be well'. By chapter 40 Julian has shifted from a theological discussion of sin to a pastoral understanding of how God tenderly looks after us, even in our sin, through the offices of confession and absolution. In one sense sin has been dealt with pastorally through forgiveness by the mercy and grace of God. We are safe, all is indeed well, but because we do not fully receive the peace and charity which comes from this forgiveness now, she writes, it is fitting for us to live with our Lord in sweet prayer and in loving longing. This passing reference to prayer is the link for Julian to introduce the next revelation, the showing which dives into the pastoral life of prayer and the role we play in God's loving and saving action in this world. But what was the life of prayer like in the 14th century and was it any different to our own?

The life of prayer

As an anchoress Julian's daily life would have been shaped and scaffolded by prayer. For centuries this life of prayer had been structured by the monastic divine office which punctuated the hours of the day with different services, all in Latin: matins, lauds, prime, terce, sext, none, vespers and compline. Along with the Mass, this daily and nightly round of prayers was required of all priests, monks and nuns by the medieval church. However, by the late 14th century more and more lay people were saying an alternative to the divine office called the Little Office of the Blessed Virgin Mary or the Hours of the Virgin, for short. It was this office which formed the core of the often beautifully illuminated books of hours of the period.

Shorter than the divine office, the Hours of the Virgin kept the same basic Latin prayers of psalms, readings from scripture, antiphons, responsories, versicles, glorias, the Creed, the Hail Mary and the Lord's Prayer, but unlike the longer monastic office it rarely changed according to the season and service. Instead, it consistently kept the same psalms and readings for each day, dispensing with the Benedictine notion of saying all the psalms in a single week. It was this office that women were particularly advised to follow, and it is therefore very possible that Julian herself used it, not only as an anchoress, but also prior to her enclosure.

In the 13th-century guide for anchoresses, the *Ancrene Wisse*, the Office of the Virgin is also mentioned but, in addition to this daily routine, the guide advises the anchoress to encase herself in prayers every moment of the day. For example, from the moment she awakes the anchoress is bidden to get up, cross herself, then say the opening sentence, 'In the name of the Father and of the Son and of the Holy Spirit', followed by a hymn. As she dresses, the Lord's Prayer, the Creed and the Jesus Prayer are to be repeated until her morning ablutions are completed, and so it continued throughout the day. We cannot say for sure whether Julian followed such minute directions. However, this possible prototype to the later development of the 13th-century book of hours gives us a good sense of the purpose of the anchoress' life. It was to pray in a strict, structured and formulaic way which was based on the corporate prayers of the church.

Like the majority of people at that time, it is very likely that, in her practice of prayer, Julian would have said her formal prayers out loud. This common practice of recitation came to have some interesting practical applications. For example, recipe books of the day often used prayers and the length of time it took to recite them as ways to mark out timings in cooking. Julian may also have used certain prayer postures similar to those used today. We know from the *Ancrene Wisse* that the anchoress was instructed to follow a number of different prayer actions: sprinkling herself with holy water, prostration, beating her breast, making a cross on the earth and kissing it, along with the attitudes we are more familiar with today, such as bowing, kneeling, standing and making the sign of the cross.

Julian lived in a time of rich expressions of prayer, but that does not mean that they went uncriticised, especially by those who saw such outward signs as easily descending into shows of devotion which lacked inner conviction. In the fifth book or *passus* of his poem *Piers Plowman*, William Langland, as the dreamer within the poem, describes how he drifted off to sleep muttering his rosary. Falling asleep during the saying of his prayers is reflected in the following dream, where he sees Reason preaching to the field of folk and trying to rouse them out of the sleep of sin.

Alongside the liturgical and extra-liturgical prayers of the book of hours there were also numerous collections of prayers known as *libelli precum*. These books gathered together individual Latin prayers attributed to major theological and patristic writers. They included prayers for use on special occasions, those to be directed to certain saints and aspects of the Trinity, as well as prayers which focused on Christ's life, especially the passion. Increasingly, though, by the late 14th and early 15th centuries, we find books of hours becoming more personalised with favourite vernacular prayers being added in the margins. These forms of prayers in English were also found in miscellaneous texts, such as household books and compilations, that drew on numerous sources. Invariably they were not prayers which were formally spoken but were seen as springboards on which to meditate and lead the person into a deeper and closer relationship with God.

Meditation and contemplation

Meditation has always been a key aspect of prayer within the Christian faith since the time of the neo-Platonic theologians, such as Origen and Gregory of Nyssa, as well as Augustine and Pseudo-Dionysius the Areopagite. It formed the basis of the monastic discipline of reading scripture known as *lectio divina*, which engaged the religious in slow meditative immersion in the holy word. But it was in the eleventh century, with the prayers and meditations of Anselm, that the practice of prayer took on a particular form and became central to the private devotion of layfolk in the medieval period.

In his letter to Countess Mathilda, Anselm sets out an intimate and intensely personal form of prayer which broke away from the formal prayers of the church and encouraged layfolk, as well as religious, to enter deeply into their relationship with God. His brief words opened up a tradition that encouraged the devout to imaginatively and emotionally engage with Christ through personal prayer. While private reading of the Bible was closed to many, the tools of holy reading, which the religious had enjoyed for hundreds of years, were made accessible to layfolk and religious alike. Anselm also encouraged Mathilda to make up her own prayers and in so doing gave credence to the inner individual expression of devotion. This way of praying became a hallmark of the period and shaped such vernacular writers as Richard Rolle and Nicholas Love in their intense meditations on the passion.

For the spiritual guides and writers of the contemplative life in the 14th century, meditation was seen as an important stepping stone on the road to contemplative prayer. Walter Hilton, whose text *The*

Scale of Perfection was written specifically for a solitary, describes meditation as the second of three means by which to attain contemplation, the others being the reading of holy scriptures and constant prayer. As they were only able to hear the Bible read in church in Latin, it was through prayer and meditation that the heart could be stripped of all earthly things and rise to know Christ.

Similarly, the author of *The Cloud of Unknowing* presents a powerful, biblical image of the ascent to contemplative prayer and love of God, for God's sake alone, in terms of entering a cloud of unknowing. To remain in this cloud of ontological being with God, he counsels that a cloud of forgetting be placed between you and all thoughts and meditations which are less than God and instead direct a naked intention of love with which to batter the cloud of unknowing. For *The Cloud of Unknowing* author, contemplative prayer is not so much an act of the imagination or intellect but rather a kind of 'seeing' which is beyond the usual activities of the mind:

> The first time you practise contemplation, you'll experience a darkness, like a cloud of unknowing. You won't know what this is… this darkness and this cloud will always be between you and your God… they will always keep you from seeing him clearly by the light of understanding in your intellect and will block you from feeling Him fully in the sweetness of love in your emotions. So be sure to make your home in this darkness… We can't think our way to God… that's why I'm willing to abandon everything I know, to love the one thing I cannot think. He can be loved, but not thought.

It is likely therefore that, whereas formal liturgical prayers of the offices were probably spoken out loud and with traditional gestures of devotion, contemplation and meditation were both an inner and a silent practice of prayer that, as a contemplative and anchoress, Julian would have been well versed in.

Julian gives us an inkling that much of her prayer life, apart from the liturgical offices, was silent. Towards the end of chapter 41, she describes how the soul is sometimes so stirred with gratitude that it 'breaks out with voice and says, "Good Lord, grant mercy; blessed may you be!"' Conversely, when the heart is dry and feels nothing, or when it is tempted, then reason drives it 'to cry out to our Lord aloud, recounting his blessed passion and his great goodness'. In these brief references Julian gives us an insight into her practice of prayer, which we largely know very little about, for in this fourteenth revelation Julian is not so much concerned with how we pray and the forms we use as with the inner state of our hearts when we turn to God in prayer.

Petitionary prayer

For those of you who are familiar with the popular network of silent, contemplative prayer groups known as the Julian Groups, it may come as quite a shock that Julian's fourteenth showing on prayer does not focus on the deep, inner experience of silent, contemplative prayer. Instead, it is about the practice of petitionary or intercessory prayer, namely the asking of requests from God on behalf of others or for ourselves. This form of prayer was often associated with the simplest and early stages of someone's prayer life. When we place the short version of Julian's text next to the later longer version, it is interesting to see just how much she builds and develops her understanding of this revelatory experience over time.

I have placed the two texts alongside each other so that you can see how she changes her text over time. The short version is in bold type, the unhighlighted text is the long version and the italic text is where her two versions coincide:

After this, our Lord gave **me** *a revelation about prayer, in which showing I saw two qualities in our Lord's meaning…*

often that I have felt myself. *Firstly,* **they will not pray for anything except that which is the will of God and to his worship. Secondly, is that they set themselves mightily and continually to beseech that which is his will and his worship. And that is the understanding I have from the teaching of holy church. For in this our Lord taught me the same: to have God's gifts of faith, hope and love and to keep ourselves in this to our lives end. And in this we say Pater Noster, Ave, and the Creed with devotion, as God's will gives. And so, we pray for all our even Cristen [the ordinary, lay believer] and for all manner of men, that is God's will. For we would that all manner of men and women were in the same vertu [virtue] and grace we ought to desire for ourselves.** *But yet* **in all this** *oftentimes our trust is not full.*

One is rightful prayer; the other is seker [sure] trust. *But oftentimes our trust is not complete. For we are not seker [sure] that God hears us, and we think ourselves unworthy and as we feel nothing at all. For we are as dry and barren oftentimes after our prayers as we were before. And so, in our sense, it is our folly that is the cause of our weakness. For so I have felt it myself.*

Both versions of the text are focused on the same pastoral concern, namely that we are unsure whether God hears us when we pray and, as a result, we are left as dry and barren of the assurance of God's presence after our time of prayer as we were before. Those who hear or give spiritual direction today will immediately resonate with this pastoral concern, for it's a problem that is as prevalent today as it was in Julian's time. In this context it is clear that Julian is using the word 'prayer' in a specifically biblical way to mean petition.

While both the texts make it clear that this concern arises from Julian's own experience of prayer, this personal statement appears in different places. Initially she has it as the defining factor in her revelation and so places it at the beginning of the chapter, but in the later text she has come to realise that this is not a personal problem in prayer but one shared by many. It has been argued that Julian's first text was primarily written for her fellow contemplatives and solitaries, whose lives would have been devoted to intercessory prayer for others. It was only later that Julian began to broaden her understanding and come to see that her revelation was meant for 'mine even Cristen' and not just for a professional group of religious. This would make sense of Julian's shift from focusing on her own experience of the life of prayer as shared by her fellow contemplatives, to understanding that this was more of a corporate concern that afflicted not only the devout, but also the laity. Perhaps it was a truth she had come to realise from the spiritual conversations she had at her anchorhold window.

Even from just a cursory glance, you can see that the short text (above in bold) has a sizable section which is excluded from the long. In this earlier version, Julian sees prayer as a process of aligning ourselves with God's love and will so that there is nothing we could ask for that is not of his will or to his worship. For Julian this alignment is possible through God's gifts of faith, hope and love, the three theological virtues described in 1 Corinthians 13 and subsequently taught by 'holy church'. Through living the life of holiness, built on virtue, our will is aligned to the love and will of God and hence, through this love, to each other. To counter the temptation of external devotion becoming hollow and just for show, Julian emphasises that it is out of this inner, spiritual life of virtue, lived in step with the love of God, that we join in the liturgical, outward prayers of the church. Julian then goes on to express the pastoral problem in terms of a lack of trust in God and the uncertainty that prayers are heard, from which results a sense of dryness and feelings of wickedness.

Julian's removal of this section radically simplifies her text to focus on the two key properties of prayer that afflict everyone and are rooted in our failure to see that we are 'kept full *sekerly*', a Middle

English word, which can be translated as 'safely' or 'securely'. As we have already noted, this showing arises from the spiritual understanding that we are all kept safe (*seker*) from sin and united to God and each other through his love. Julian's long text picks up the words that closed chapter 40, the words which gave great reassurance, namely, that we are kept securely. Julian then repeats them in the following chapter. In this long version it is the word 'safe', or *'seker'*, which becomes the defining property of prayer. Through our trust in prayer we are thereby kept safe within the loving, saving presence of God. Into the folly of this simple misconception Christ then speaks to her, giving her words of comfort and insight which will keep all 'even Cristen' in the knowledge that they have no reason to doubt as they are *kept full sekerly*.

Ground of your beseeching

It is at this point that Julian inserts the words of Christ which are the core of the showing:

> 'I am the ground of your beseeching: first it is my will that you have it and since I make you to will it, and since I make you to beseech it and you do beseech it, how should it then be that you should not have your beseeching?' And thus, in the first statement, along with the three that follow, our good lord shewed me a mighty comfort, as it may be seen in the same words.

Both the long and the short text reflect each other as they quote these words verbatim, revealing how they formed for Julian the content of the showing of the fourteenth revelation. Central to this revelation are the opening words: 'I am the ground of thy beseeching', which translates as 'I am the foundation of your prayers.' Christ's statements which follow qualify what these words mean.

Once the revelatory words are concluded, Julian systematically breaks them down into individual parts and places alongside them their different meanings to form a list. For ease I have listed each one with the verse and then the 'reason', as she calls it:

First reason: 'I am the foundation of your prayers' – 'in the first reason and the following three the Lord showed a mighty comfort'

Second reason: 'it is my will that thou should have something'

Third reason: 'then I make you desire it'

Fourth reason: 'then I make you pray for it'

Fifth reason: 'and if you pray for it!' – 'there he shows the very great pleasure and endless reward that he will give us in prayer'

Sixth reason: 'how then could it be' – 'this is an impossibility, for how can we pray for mercy and grace and not have them'

At this point the short text returns to the question of the lack of trust we have, but the long text again erases this and instead adds in a section which explains that it is out of God's goodness, and not through our asking, that God gives us mercy and grace.

In this way Julian shifts the onus from being focused on us and how we should pray only according to God's will, to placing the onus on God himself, who is the foundation and fount of all our prayers. It is not we who pray to God, asking our particular petitions and intercessions, but God who prays through us. This is a much firmer foundation on which to trust, rather than on whether our prayers are correct or not. Walter Hilton expresses the same truth about the nature of prayer in chapter 4 of the first book of his *The Scale of Perfection*:

For though it be so, that prayer is not the cause for which our Lord gives grace, nevertheless it is a way or means by which grace freely given comes into a soul.

This is very different from the prevalent idea that God hears only his friends and will grant them those reasonable things that they ask because they only prayer as God wills.

Prayer unites the soul with God

Having peeled away the layers of meaning to the revelation, Julian then goes on to the heart of what intercessory prayer really is:

Intercessory prayer is a true, grace-inspired, enduring act of the soul, united and fastened to the will of our Lord by the sweet, secret work of the Holy Ghost.

In these beautiful words, intercessory prayers are not seen as primarily vocal prayers that are used by layfolk in their simple, active engagement with God, but rather Julian incorporates them into the secret work of the mystical prayer of solitaries and those seemingly advanced in the life of prayer.

For Julian, all prayer, whether it be vocal or silent, intercessory or contemplative, corporate or alone, is part of the secret work of the Holy Spirit that unites us to God and keeps us safe. In this way Julian re-visions Paul's words to the church in Rome:

Likewise the Spirit helps us in our weakness. For we do not know what to pray for as we ought, but the Spirit himself intercedes for us with groanings too deep for words. And he who searches hearts knows what is the mind of the Spirit, because the Spirit intercedes for the saints according to the will of God.

ROMANS: 8:26–27 (ESV)

In a rather remarkable comment for its time, Julian continues in this mystical understanding of intercessory prayer as she states that:

> Our lord himself receives our prayer first, as I saw it, and accepts it gratefully. And highly rejoicing he sends it above and sets it in his treasury where it shall never perish.

Julian is clearly echoing the words of Matthew 6:20, where Christ exhorts his followers to 'store up for yourselves treasures in heaven, where moths and vermin do not destroy, and where thieves do not break in and steal'. In a world where intercessory prayers were more often directed to Mary, the saints or the angels than they were to Christ, the intimacy of this act by Jesus is startling.

In the late 14th century, the image of treasure also had theological and ecclesiological connotations in relation to the saving work of Christ. With its roots in Anselm's doctrine of atonement, it was used to refer to the meritorious qualities of Christ's precious passion, which bestowed pardon on the penitent soul and released them from the debt of pain. Anselm understood Jesus' obedience and death as being a satisfaction for the disobedience of Adam at the Fall, thereby restoring the relationship of honour and justice between God and his creation. As the Good Friday hymn expresses, 'There was no other good enough to pay the price of sin.' Traditionally, it was through the church that the treasure of Christ's atoning blood was made available to the penitent. The early 14th-century, extremely popular penitential poem *Pricke of Conscience*, for instance, describes the church as the storehouse of the meritorious treasure of Christ, which 'is gathered for the use of pardon, by virtue of Christ's passion'. Along with the prayers and deeds of the faithful, which are the fruit of the work of the church, Christ's saving passion is held within the church. As the author of the *Pricke of Conscience* writes: 'So large is holy church's treasury that it is enough to pay thereby for all the pains that debt may be for all the men of Christianity.'

Julian similarly sees the prayers of the faithful as being held in a treasury before God. In the fullness of time, we will enter into bliss, and the joy we will have there will be proportionate to the prayers that we made on earth, and which Christ has stored in his treasury of worship for us. In Julian's eyes these prayers are not simply a payment for sin along with Christ's atoning blood, which can then be meted out and governed by the church, but they make us like Christ in restoring the image of God in us which has been effaced by the fall and sin. In a small but astounding sentence Julian incorporates our simple intercessory and petitionary prayers into the atoning work of Christ. It is through them, as much as through his blood, that we are restored, forgiven and receive joy in heaven, because our prayers do not come from us but from Christ praying through and within us.

It is in relation to this vision of the significance of petitionary and intercessory prayer before God that Julian turns once more to the problem of dryness and barrenness in prayer. Jesus speaks to her once again exhorting her and us to:

> Pray wholeheartedly: though it seems to you no pleasure, yet it is profitable enough, though you do not feel it. Pray wholeheartedly: though you feel nothing, though you see nothing, though you think you would rather not. For in dryness and barrenness, in sickness and in weakness, then is your prayer most pleasing to me, though you think it gives but little pleasure. And so is all your living prayer in my sight.

Grounded in Paul's words to the church in Thessalonica to pray continually, Julian counsels us to pray, however we are feeling, for the eagerness with which God wants to receive our prayers.

Going deeper

Spend some time slowly reading and thinking about Julian's words:

I am the foundation of your prayers.

What do these words mean for you?

What do you find difficult about prayer and why?

What do you think Jesus would say to you?

Laying aside your inner thoughts and feelings, be still in the presence of Jesus and rest in his loving arms.

What will you take away with you from this time of meditation?

Questions to ponder

- What is prayer for you?
- Does Julian's description of intercessory prayer change or deepen your understanding of prayer?
- What is your rhythm of prayer?
- How would you encourage someone in their prayer life?
- What would you say to someone who says prayer is pointless?

Words for the journey

Do not be anxious about anything, but in everything by prayer and supplication with thanksgiving let your requests be made known to God.

PHILIPPIANS 4:6 (ESV)

THE FIFTEENTH REVELATION

– 8 –

PATIENT SUFFERING

Julian turns to the pastoral issue of how we live in the world, where clearly all is not well – where pain and suffering continue despite the love and revelation of Christ to the contrary. Her revelation does not escape into a mystical realm; rather it stays rooted in this world and the truths that are learnt on the pilgrim path of yearning and patient endurance, which takes us as much through sunlit hills of joy as it does dark forests of sorrow. Julian's vision reveals that there will be a day when we are lifted from the mire of this world into the full presence of God. Then we will see and know that through the secret work of Christ we have been kept safe in 'wele and woe' and he has worked all things to our good.

Julian's fifteenth showing in her *Revelations of Divine Love* springs out of her 'longing and desire by God's grace to be delivered of this world and of this life'. This may seem a rather morbid sentiment to have, even in an age when life was short and many had witnessed the horrors of the Black Death. Yet it was a common feature of meditative, devotional writing of the time which goes back to Paul's articulation of his 'desire to depart and be with Christ, which is better by far' (Philippians 1:23). In this statement Julian sends us right back to the first passionate devotional desires of her youth which she wrote about in chapter 2 of the *Revelations of Divine Love*. Her desire 'to soon be with her Lord' formed a key aspect of Julian's initial wish to receive three gifts from God. Along with having mind of Christ's passion and to receive three wounds, Julian also wished to have a bodily sickness which was:

So serious as to seem mortal, so that in this illness I might receive all the rites of holy church, myself believing that I should die, and that all creatures might believe the same who see me, for I would have no manner of comfort in this earthly life. In this sickness I desired to have all manner of bodily and spiritual pains that I would have as if I were to die, with all the dreads and tempests of the devils, short of the passing of the soul. And in this I meant for to be purged by the grace of God and afterwards live more to the worship of God because of that sickness; and that it might assist me in my death, for I desired to soon be with my God.

The key aspect of this passage is not so much Julian's wish to die, but rather to live more to the worship of God. It is true that those people who have come close to death, in any form, often express the extent to which their lives have been changed by it. Perhaps it prompts a desire to live a life of deeper meaning than they had before or it has bestowed on them a profound sense that every moment matters. Either way, something has fundamentally changed. Julian would identify this with living a life more to the worship of God. We may not name it in such religious terms, but the Covid pandemic similarly resulted in a societal shift which reflected this desire, where many people changed jobs, retrained or simply retired early to seek a life of more significance. Julian tells us that this second desire soon passed from her mind, so why does she suddenly remember it now at chapter 64 of her text?

The answer to this question is found in the positioning of this showing within the body of her writing. The description of the fifteenth showing occurs 23 chapters after the fourteenth showing on prayer. Within the text the showings have played less and less of a defining and shaping role for Julian's writing, as her thinking and interpretation of them have broadened out into the areas of human nature, sin and the work of God within the world through the motherhood of Christ and the sustaining work of the Holy Spirit. In the previous chapter, Julian reached the culmination of her thinking and exploration on Jesus' words that 'all shall be well', which began in the thirteenth revelation. This has led to the final understanding that we cannot fully know now how all shall be well but must trust in the secret work of God. It will only be when we are gathered up into God that we will understand his sweet words which said:

'All shall be well, and you shall see it yourself that all manner of thing shall be well.' And then the bliss of our motherhood in Christ will begin anew in the joys of our God; a new beginning which will last without end, always beginning anew.

Until that time, Julian realises that we shall only ever be as children in our weakness and need of our mother Christ to bear us to the Father.

It is following this heavenly vision of when all the secrets will be revealed that Julian has been reminded of her first youthful prayer and desire to be rid of this world and all its sufferings and be with Christ in his bliss right now.

For often I beheld the sorrow that is here and the joy and bliss that is being there. As if there had been no pain in this life but the absence of our lord, methought it was sometimes more than I might bare; and this made me to mourn and intently yearn, as did also my own wretchedness, sloth and weakness, that I wished not to live and to work as it fell to me to do.

The theme of *wele,* or joy, and woe has run throughout the revelations, right from the moment when Julian, in her extreme illness, looked at the cross held before her eyes and was suddenly lifted out of pain, to a profound expression of the dichotomy of the joys in heaven and the pains on earth. Julian lived through the bubonic plague of the Black Death, and we cannot overestimate the suffering she must have witnessed by those who were afflicted with this horrendous disease. She may well have had firsthand experience of watching her family succumb to its lethal effects. But Julian is thinking not just about the physical woes of this short life; to her what is unbearable is the sense of the absence of God, that absence which her last showing touched upon in relation to the dryness of prayer. Just as in the second showing, where Julian suddenly switched from a time of visionary insight into dark doubts about whether her revelations were true, so here in the fifteenth showing Julian plummets from an ecstatic state of joy and insight into the depths of suffering and despair at a perceived sense of the absence of God. In this awareness of her sin, even her longing to be with Christ is turned into a self-loathing desire to be rid of this world.

Words of comfort

Once again it is out of a pastoral and devotional concern that Julian's showing flows. In the previous showing, the fourteenth, the pastoral concern was focused on prayer and the fear that God did not hear the prayers of the devout. Now in the fifteenth, she cries out from the mire in her desperation at the sense of the absence of God and the sin that 'clings so closely', as the author of the letter to the Hebrews expresses it. Picking up the sense of a loss of comfort that the servant experiences in chapter 51, Jesus does not so much answer a question or a concern as to speak words of comfort into Julian's despairing and turbulent spiritual state when he says:

> Suddenly you shall be taken from all your pain, from all your sickness, from all your discomfort, from all your woe. And you shall come up above, and you shall have me as your reward, and you shall be fulfilled with joy and bliss. And you shall never more have any kind of pain, any kind of sickness, any kind of displeasure, any frustration of your desire, but always joy and bliss. What should it then aggrieve you to suffer a while, since it is to my will and my worship.

The use of the double negatives in the Middle English text, 'never… no… no… no', sound like the yearning reassurances of a lover, seeking to comfort his beloved with words of promise to Julian. He is emphatic that the pain, sorrow, sickness and woe will come to an end, even though it does not feel like it for Julian. Instead, Julian realises that what lies behind his words of comfort can be summed up in the single term 'patience'.

Patience is a virtue

I guess most of us know the value of patience through its opposite, impatience. There's nothing like being trapped in a traffic jam, trying to get to an important meeting, or the food never arriving at a restaurant, or even being a child on Christmas eve, to know exactly what impatience feels like. In these times of annoyance and frustration we can easily descend into that age-old vice of anger.

Back in the fifth century, in his poem 'Psychomachia', Prudentius first allegorised the Christian life as one of a struggle between the figures of virtue and vice. While these may not have much bearing on the seven deadly or capital sins and their equivalent virtues, which were to follow, they set the moral tone of how to understand the inner workings of the human heart and how we can define sin. These capital or remedial virtues differ from the cardinal virtues, which are the four virtues of the mind– prudence, justice, fortitude and temperance – as well as the three theological virtues– faith, hope and love – which together make the seven heavenly virtues. It was Pope Gregory in 590 who revised Prudentius' list and set out the ranking of the capital virtues and vices, also known as the remedial or contrary virtues to the seven deadly sins, which we are more familiar with today:

Virtue	Vice
Humility	Pride
Chastity	Lust
Temperance	Guttony
Kindness	Envy
Charity	Avarice
Diligence	Sloth
Patience	Anger

As you can see in this list the opposing virtue to the vice of anger is patience. Patience is the virtue which undoes the effect of anger and brings back equilibrium within us and with God. But what does it mean to be patient, to wait?

In his letter James writes:

> Be patient, then, brothers and sisters, until the Lord's coming. See how the farmer waits for the land to yield its valuable crop, patiently waiting for the autumn and spring rains. You too, be patient and stand firm, because the Lord's coming is near.
> JAMES 5:7–8

You don't have to be a farmer or even a gardener to know that a precious crop of potatoes, sprouts and cauliflower won't suddenly appear once you plant the seed in the ground. It takes sunshine, rain and time for the vegetables to come up in due season. It takes time and patience. No amount of annoyance, frustration or anger will make it grow any quicker. But it will come, just as the spring will follow the winter.

Patience not only helps us to be grounded in the present, but also enables us to see the value and gift of the present time rather than wishing after the future. In the natural world patience helps us enjoy the winter days as well as the summer ones; the stately majesty of the tree branches stripped of leaves, the mornings of crisp frost and clear light, the buds of promise and first tender flowers. Patience opens the eternal door to the present moment which we can easily dismiss or pass over in our impatience for a better time. It has the potential to show us that there is value in the hard times of suffering as well as the days and experiences of joy and visionary ecstasy.

James also intimates in his letter that there is another dimension to patience which can be harder and more painful. He writes:

> Don't grumble against one another, brothers and sisters, or you will be judged. The Judge is standing at the door! Brothers and sisters, as an example of patience in the face of suffering, take the prophets who spoke in the name of the Lord. As you know, we count as blessed those who have persevered. You have heard of Job's perseverance and have seen what the Lord finally brought about. The Lord is full of compassion and mercy.
> JAMES 5:9–11

In the *Oxford English Dictionary*, the word patience is defined as 'the capacity to accept or tolerate delay, problems, or suffering without becoming annoyed or anxious'. Waiting for spring is one thing; accepting problems without being annoyed is another. That's why patience is listed as one of the fruits of the Holy Spirit by Paul in Galatians 5:22–23, because we cannot do it alone but need God to give us his gift of patience to help us in our waiting. For James, the icon of this patient endurance is Job seated upon his dung heap, defiant to all who would urge him to 'curse God and die' (Job 2:9). But Job is insistent that he is innocent of wrongdoing and endures and perseveres with God even in the midst of his suffering.

1 The quatrefoil and squint windows from the anchorhold at St James'
Church, Shere

2 Detail of the enclosure of an anchoress

3 Life-size wound and Man of Sorrows from a 14th-century French book of hours

4 Crucifixion page from The Sherbourne Missal

5 The East window depicting the Virgin Mary with the Christ Child in
St Michael and All Angels, Eaton Bishop Herefordshire

6 IHS monogram from the Despencer Retable, Norwich Cathedral

7 Confession panel on the Seven Sacrament font, St John's Baptist,
Badingham, Suffolk

8 Woodcut from a German block-book edition of 'ars moriendi'
1471; angels vying with and triumphing over demons for the soul of a
dying man

9 Detail from the Trinity Apocalypse of the new Jerusalem

10 Detail from the Trinity Apocalypse of water flowing from the throne of the Lord and the Lamb

The patience of God

In the opening of the wonderful 14th-century Middle English poem entitled 'Patience' we read these wise words:

Patience is a princely thing, though displeasing often.
When heavy hearts are scorned, or otherwise hurt,
Sufferance may assuage and soothe the searing pain:
It subdues dire evil and does away with malice.

For when a man bears woe, he wins joy later,
But, fretting at misfortune, he feels it more forcefully:
So better it is to bear the blow in due time
Than express my impatience, in spite of the pain.

Ironically, the rest of the poem goes on to recount – in alliterative verse – the tale not of Job but of Jonah, perhaps one of the most impatient figures in the Bible. It's not Jonah, though, who epitomises patience in this poem but God. It is God who patiently waits and hears Jonah's grumbling and moaning, his impatience with a gourd and his laments of suffering inside the whale. All these God patiently bears with until at the end of the poem God says to him:

'Be less furious, my fine fellow and fare you forth!
Be brave and forbearing in bitterness and joy,
For he who rashly rages and rips his clothes
Must then sit with the torn stuff and sew it together.'

So when Poverty oppresses me with pains in plenty,
It shall become me in quiet and calm to suffer;
In pain and in penance to prove plainly
That Patience is a princely thing, though displeasing often.

The poem beautifully expresses how impatience invariably is self-inflicted suffering, the tearing of one's own clothes and then having to stitch them together.

This idea is dramatically and horrifyingly expressed in Dante's *Inferno,* where the poet comes across the sin of anger in two forms, the wrathful and sullen in the fifth circle of hell. As with many of the punishments of Dante's depiction of hell, those who are afflicted with anger create their own hellish place. The wrathful beat themselves in frustration and fight with one another, while the sullen stew below the surface of a muddy swamp which consumes them forever. It is comforting to know that, like Jonah, God bears patiently with us, pouring on us his gift of patience that, whether in *wele* or woe, we may more patiently bear with ourselves and with one another. Jesus speaks to Julian words not only of comfort but also of patience. We are to emulate Christ in the way we patiently bear with times of suffering as he patiently bore the sufferings of the cross and the muddy *slade.*

A body and a little child

Julian's vision now shifts from the form of locution into that of a bodily sight as the imagery and experience of the sin along with Christ's words are visualised into a showing of a little child rising from a swollen, heaving mass of stinking mire:

> At this time, I saw a body lying on the earth, a body which looked heavy and ugly, without shape or form as if it were a swollen, heaving mass of stinking mire. And suddenly out of this body there sprang a full fair creature, a little child fully shaped and formed, quick and alive and whiter than a lily, which glided swiftly up into heaven. And the swelling of the body signified the great wretchedness of our mortal flesh, and the littleness of the child signified the cleanness of the purity in the soul.

In this bodily vision Julian is not necessarily following the prevalent thinking of the time, which separated the body from the soul, where the body is seen as the flesh full of sin and the soul as a child or perfect image of God within us. Instead, Julian's vision reflects, in a visual form, both her desire to be rid of this world and her spiritual sense of being trapped within a state of sin, which is experienced as an ugly, swollen bog. Just as the pure child in her vision was released from the mire, so Julian longs to be lifted out of the dirt and rise to heaven pure and clean, without any of the mud or sin still sticking to her.

In many ways Julian's visualisation of her state of despair echoes that of Psalm 68 in the Douay Rheims English translation of the Latin Vulgate, or 69 in the later King James Version of the Bible. Here, in a psalm that is often used on Good Friday, the psalmist cries out to God:

> Save me, O God; for the waters are come in unto my soul.
> I sink in deep mire, where there is no standing: I am come into
>   deep waters, where the floods overflow me.
> I am weary of my crying: my throat is dried: mine eyes fail while
>   I wait for my God.
> PSALM 69:1–3 (KJV)

This sense of the deep mire is also theologically expressed by Julian in the example of the lord and the servant in chapter 51, where the servant, in his haste to do the will of the lord, tumbles into a *slade* and there through his weakness and suffering is no longer able to see the loving gaze of the lord.

The Middle English word *'slade'* beautifully expresses the notion that the servant has fallen into the earthy landscape of this world. It can be translated in a number of different ways, including hollow, chasm, valley and slough, but perhaps the best translation is that of the biblical 'mire', as this graphic term captures the sense in which the servant is trapped within a dangerous boggy place, unable to get out and caked in filth, as expressed by the psalmist. Julian's use of similar language connects the servant's fall into the mire with her own spiritual experience of the absence of God. In both cases it is the inability to see the loving gaze of the lord for his servant, this isolation, that causes the greatest physical as well as spiritual hurt.

Julian's bodily sight of a lily-white child being drawn out of a 'heaving mass of stinking mire' also echoes later verses from Psalm 69. Here the psalmist writes:

> Deliver me out of the mire, and let me not sink; let me be delivered from them that hate me, and out of the deep waters.
> PSALM 69:14 (KJV)

This biblical idea of being rescued runs as a thread through scripture and theological tradition, from Adam formed of the mud of the earth through to the harrowing of hell, where Christ hauls the first fathers and mothers out of the pit of death. For the devotional writers of the late 14th century, the imagery of the swollen, heaving mass sings with resonances of their experience of sin and how to deal with it. This is especially found in *The Cloud of Unknowing*, written by an unknown Carthusian in the same period as Julian. Drawing on the ideas of the penitential literature, *The Cloud of Unknowing* author gives his young disciple a few tricks and techniques to help him cope with sinful stirrings or past sins that weigh heavy on his mind. One of these is to know when to cower before these stirrings and surrender yourself to the help of God:

> Knowing and feeling yourself as you are, a wretch and a lump of dirt far worse than nothing.

He goes on to advise his pupil to 'focus on sin as a lump' and to use the word 'sin' to embody all that you wish to flee from or that divides you from God. Like Julian, the *Cloud* author does not demark sin into the various types and species, but instead all sins are lumped into a swollen mass from which sinful thoughts and stirrings spring up.

For Julian what emerges from, or should I say is released from, this swollen mass of sin, takes the form of a child. It would be easy to associate this lily-white figure with the soul and see it being released from the vile body of the flesh on death. Many illustrations of death at this time depicted the soul as a lily-white child, not least the long tradition of representing the dormition of Mary in terms of Christ cradling her soul as a swaddled baby as he stands over the gently sleeping corpse of his mother. While there are certainly resonances with this imagery of death, for Julian there is also the sense in which this is a new birth and the true nature of the person is being reborn, released into that close relationship with God which is only fully realised when we die.

——— *Going deeper* ———

Spend some time slowly reading and thinking about Julian's words:

> Suddenly you shall be taken from all your pain, from all your sickness, from all your discomfort, from all your woe. And you shall come up above, and you shall have me as your reward, and you shall be fulfilled with joy and bliss. And you shall never more have any kind of pain, any kind of sickness, any kind of displeasure, any frustration of your desire, but always joy and bliss. What should it then aggrieve you to suffer a while, since it is to my will and my worship.

What word or phrase are you drawn to?

Ponder it for a moment, gently turning it over in your mind.

Gradually become aware of God's presence with you.

Listen with the ear of your heart to what he wishes to say to you.

Instead of trying to silence your inner thoughts and feelings, let them float by like the flowing water of a stream and allow your attention to go deeper into silence.

What will you take away from this time of contemplation?

Questions to ponder

- How does Julian's vision give a new perspective on suffering?
- What does the word patience evoke for you?
- Thinking of a time when you have been patient and a time when you have been impatient, what do you learn about yourself from them?
- In what ways does Julian's vision of sin as a mire assist you in your spiritual journey?
- What words of comfort would you give to someone who is dying?

Words for the journey

Be still before the Lord and wait patiently for him; fret not yourself over the one who prospers in his way, over the man who carries out evil devices! Refrain from anger, and forsake wrath! Fret not yourself; it only tends to evil.

PSALM 37:7–9 (ESV)

THE SIXTEENTH REVELATION

– 9 –

TRIALS AND TRIBULATIONS

Julian sets the scene for her final revelation, the vision of the Christ seated within the soul. She recalls how her vision was preceded by a time of diabolical temptation. In this vulnerable place, suspended between this life and the next, the devil comes intent to destroy her trust and ridicule her revelations. But Julian cannot forget what she has seen and the promise that Jesus gave her that in the end all manner of things shall be well. With words of praise on her lips and the faith of holy church in her heart she breaks through the mountain mist of despair and self-loathing to arrive at the peak of the last revelation.

We have come at last to the final showing in Julian's sixteen visions which made up the one revelation of love. Julian's use of two rhetorical terms, 'conclusion' and 'confirmation', to describe this sixteenth showing would immediately have notified the medieval reader that this final vision is the peroration of her work – that is, it sums up and encapsulates the meaning of all that has gone before. Right at this point of climax and ending, Julian suddenly pulls us out of the visionary realm by stating: 'But first I need to tell you about my weakness, wretchedness and blindness.' Driven by a sense of necessity, Julian returns us to 1373 and that narrow space of her sick bed where a woman lay dying. We have leapt from discursive, visionary mode back to descriptive mode as Julian recounts the events which took place just before her final showing.

Chapter 66 in the British Library Sloane manuscript of the *Revelations of Divine Love*, and the equivalent chapters in the Paris manuscript, act in terms of a flashback, as the pain that Julian had been released from during the previous fifteen showings now returns with a vengeance. Julian's physical bodily illness is echoed by an inner 'ghostly' sickness as she experiences what John of the Cross would later describe as the 'dark night of the soul', an overwhelming sense of feebleness and blindness as well as desolation. For the *Cloud* author it is this experience of the darkness of God, or the place of the cloud of unknowing, where the contemplative must dwell if they are to know God as he is in himself.

Once again, a religious person is called for to give spiritual aid and comfort. This person would probably have been a member of a religious community, given the words that Julian uses to describe them, possibly a friar or canon of the secular orders. Julian tells us that she dismissed her revelation to him as the mad ravings of delirium. The religious person initially laughs them off but when Julian begins to articulate the revelation to him the mood changes and the religious person suddenly becomes very serious, astounded at her words. As if to emphasise this act of articulation, Julian gives us the words she spoke verbatim: 'The cross that stood before my face, methought it bled fast.' Bleeding crosses were not unknown during this period, so Julian would not have been saying anything unique. But on seeing how seriously the religious person takes her first few tentative attempts to articulate her vision, Julian deeply repents of her betrayal of Christ who had given her these visions.

Looking back at this encounter, Julian now realises what a weak and blinded state she had been in. She even uses the same words to describe her experience as that of the servant trapped in the mire who moans and groans in the sufferings of sin and his inability to see the loving gaze of the lord. With a searing sense of shame Julian now sees how she had cut herself off from Christ and the comfort that her revelation had given her. Full of contrition Julian wished to be shriven but was unable to confess and receive the forgiveness which would bring her peace. It is clear that, while the religious person had come to see how she was doing, he was not a priest or her confessor and so was unable to give the sacrament of reconciliation. Julian closes this encounter with the religious person with the words: 'Here may you see what I am in myself; but our courteous Lord would not leave me like this.'

It is at this point that Julian describes how she fell asleep. What followed was a dream, or should I say a nightmare, in which she was visited by a devil who sat at her throat and leered into her face. Julian is very careful to mark out this diabolical episode as a dream and not a vision, even though it is a very vivid dream. She woke momentarily in a fever and those around her wetted her fevered brow, but she was still in a state of abject fear and believed she smelt smoke, the smoke of devilish brimstone, coming into the room. Crying out 'Blessed be God' at this temptation by the devil, she immediately realised that all her showings had been true and, along with the faith of 'holy church', accepted them. At once the nightmare faded and she received great rest and peace without any sickness in her body or dread of conscience.

Diabolical temptations

From the time of Jesus' temptations in the wilderness, the Christian spiritual tradition has always been aware that when we intentionally seek to turn to God and live a life of holiness, we must first face the inner stirrings of our own heart. These stirrings, however, have invariably been articulated in an external form as demonic. The Desert Fathers and Mothers of the third and fourth century, who went into the wilderness to search for God, were confronted by fiends and temptations just as Jesus was. The fourth-century writer Evagrius of Ponticus, in his book *On Prayer*, warns everyone who wishes to pray that they will enter a battleground where demons not only try to excite sin within the soul, but also fill the head with thoughts that will seek to stop them from their prayers. They even had the potential to bring strange fantasies to the mind and make one think that they were divine visitations. Richard Rolle in the late 14th century uses the words of 2 Corinthians 11:14 to warn his solitary disciples that the devil comes disguised as an angel of light.

For the faithful of the medieval period the cosmic battle for the human soul was a daily reality which could be distilled into specific moments. One of these was around illness. In *The Chastising of God's Children*, an anonymous Middle English devotional text from around the 1390s written for women solitaries as a guide to discernment and temptations, the writer describes how the devil has power to afflict the soul through bodily infirmities and illusions. Given that Julian has just dismissed her revelation in such terms, it is therefore not surprising to her that affliction comes in the form of the devil who attempts to strangle her. As Nicholas Watson points out in his commentary on the text, Julian's description of the devil not only evokes household items that Julian would have known but is also a parody of Christ's face from the first and eighth showings. So, she describes his face as the colour of red like 'the tile stone when it is new burnt with black spots like freckles' from the soot and grease marks. The description 'his hair was red as rust, trimmed at the front, with side locks hanging down his temples' apes Christ's hair and blood hanging like a garland in chapter 17.

Another of these moments in life when the soul was seen as being highly vulnerable to assaults from the devil was centred around the sacrament of penance, especially at the moment of the last rites. On the 15th-century 'seven sacraments' font in St John the Baptist's in Badingham, Suffolk, we find a depiction of the sacrament of penance on one of the seven sides of the font (see Plate 7). It shows the external practice of confession with the priest cowled and seated on a pew in judgement, his hand raised in blessing. Before him kneels the penitent. The stonemason has caught the moment of absolution, while the internal struggle and moral significance of this moment is represented by an angel who dominates the scene, along with a horned devil ready to seize the soul if the confession is not full or true. Julian's description of her response to the religious person reflects this same state of inner torment and desolation. She too was in just such a vulnerable spiritual situation, wishing to be shriven but unable to do so. It was therefore a traditional time that was seen as ripe for the devil to appear and tempt her away from belief in her revelation and trust in the loving gaze of her Lord.

The other crucial moment in a medieval person's life, when it was believed that they were most in peril of being tempted by the devil to despair and to doubt God's love, was at the hour of death. During the medieval period and especially later into the 15th century, there was increasing anxiety about the state of the soul at this fatal moment in one's life. Once the last rites had been given, the soul was understood to be in a state of grace, but before death the soul could still sin. It was then, in this in-between time, that the devil could still snatch them away into hell and heaven be lost. The 'art of dying' texts, which became prevalent in the 15th century, taught how one could die well but also how to ensure that salvation was not lost in an instant.

This moment was often depicted as a lily-white miniature person or soul rising from a decaying body, much like Julian describes in her fifteenth vision. Striking images, like the one from Meister von Heiligenkreuz, which dates from 1425, shows the emaciated, decaying mass of the dying body while a small white childlike soul rises about it. The words which come from his mouth are: *'In manus tuas dominus…* Into your hands O Lord, I commend my spirit. For you have redeemed me, O Lord God of truth.' These are the words of Psalm 31:5 and the final words of Christ on the cross. They also form the responsory in the night office of Compline. While the devil and an angel fight for possession of the soul, the dying man frantically grips the teaching of holy church, depicted as a scroll emitting from the mouth of God.

These *ars moriendi,* or manuals on preparing for a good death, were later made into woodcuts which became extremely popular. They sought to show the spiritual world or truth behind this moment of crisis, not to evoke fear so much as to give reassurance and an explanation to the fears surrounding death. In one woodcut from the 15th century, a dying man is participating in the last rites (see Plate 8). He looks at the cross, but behind the small crucifix is the actual cross on which Christ died to make satisfaction for sin. Demons in the form of animals claw at the bed sheets, but his soul is safe in the hands of angels.

It is interesting to remember that as a result of her extreme illness, Julian had herself taken the last rites immediately before she received her revelation. She was in that state of grace, that in-between time from the ritual cleansing until her expected death, and it was during this period that she received her revelations. She was therefore in the very state which the *ars moriendi* texts highlighted as a dangerous time for the soul. In her fifteenth vision there was no battle between good and evil, an angel and the devil, but it was now just before the sixteenth vision that the devil came to tempt her with horrific imaginings and fearful reminders of hellfire and brimstone. Just like that man in the woodcut, Julian has her eyes on the cross of Christ. In confidence she cries out, 'Blessed be God', as she remembers her revelation and the teaching of 'holy church'. Just as quickly as the temptations came, so they depart and immediately, as she is affirmed in her faith, Julian is 'brought to great rest and peace without any sickness of body or dread of conscience'. Like the lily-white child of the previous showing, Julian was lifted, rescued even, from the swollen, stinking mess of sinfulness and fear to be aware once more of the loving gaze of God. Indeed, the Lord had never left her, even though for a while her faith, trust and love had been shaken and the loving gaze of the Lord hidden from her eyes.

Going deeper

Allow the words of the chapter to linger in your mind.

What thoughts, images and ideas have stood out for you? Ponder them, turning them over in your mind.

Holding these in your mind, read Julian's words again:

> Here may you see what I am in myself; but our courteous Lord, would not leave me like this.

Laying aside your inner thoughts and feelings, be still with the Lord who will not abandon or leave you.

What will you take away with you from this time of meditation?

Questions to ponder

- How can we understand the demonic language of Julian and the Bible today?
- When have you felt yourself to be tempted?
- Why does God allow us to go through a time of trial?
- How do we know that God will not leave us?
- What would you say to someone who is struggling with doubt and fears in their faith life?

Words for the journey

> Into your hand I commit my spirit; You have redeemed me,
> O Lord God of truth.
>
> PSALM 31:5 (NKJV)

– 10 –

THE CITY OF THE SOUL

Julian comes to the final vision in her revelations of love. The journey of the showings ends in a city where Christ resides as king, bishop and lord. Based on the biblical imagery, this city is found deep within the human heart. It is here that the Trinity, in Christ Jesus our Saviour, endlessly dwells, worshipfully ruling and governing all things. We may not pierce the heavens to know the secrets of God, but in this final showing Julian reveals how, out of love, Christ constantly works within the midst of our lives now, keeping us safe and ensuring that even in the midst of trials we are never overcome.

Julian did not die from her illness, and it is most likely she entered the anchorhold attached to the parish church of St Julian soon after her recovery. Once again, she went through the ritual of the last rites to be incarcerated or entombed into a relatively small room for life. Julian's life as an anchoress was therefore to dwell and pray in that in-between place, the tomb of Holy Saturday, suspended between the passion and resurrection of Christ. Julian's initial wish was indeed granted, as she came to live in that place and manner which was not just more to the worship of God, but wholly so.

It was also in a state of 'great rest and peace without sickness of body or dread of conscience' that she received her final showing, the culmination of all that has gone before.

And then our Lord opened my spiritual eye and showed me my soul in the midst of my heart. I saw the soul so large as it were an endless world and as it were a blissful kingdom; and from the conditions I saw therein I understood that it is a worshipful city. In the midst of that city sits our Lord Jesus, both God and man, a fair person and of great stature, highest bishop, noblest king and honourable lord; and I saw him solemnly and worshipfully clad. He sits in the soul even so in peace and rest. And the Godhead rules and takes care of heaven and earth and all that is, sovereign might, sovereign wisdom, and sovereign goodness. The place that Jesus takes in our soul, he shall never be removed from without end as to my sight; for in us is his homeliest home and his endless dwelling.

Julian gives us a stunning vision of the closeness of God to his beloved servant. This is not a remote lord who dwells in a far-off heavenly kingdom and looks down on his poor afflicted fallen servant struggling with the experiences of life. Rather Julian presents us with an image that reveals just how close and interconnected we are with God through Jesus Christ. It is an affirmation that, whatever state of sin we might be in, the Lord will ever be with us. It is thus the ultimate vision of our salvation and the assurance that, through and in Christ, all is well.

If we look more closely at the language and images Julian uses to describe this final vision, we find that they are replete with echoes of her previous showings, as well as with biblical and devotional expressions of God's profound relationship with humanity through Christ. In the opening image, Julian is given a vision of the inner reality of her soul in the midst of her heart. In this movement within we are immediately taken back to the tenth showing, the initial vision which marked the shift from showings focused on the passion to those which began her journey into the visions of salvation. In this tenth showing, Jesus gestures to the wound on his side and invites Julian to enter into it to find there a 'fair delightful place, large enough for all mankind that shall be saved to rest in peace and love'.

There she sees not only a place where the sinner can find safety, but also the cloven heart of Christ who pours out his blood and water in a great act of self-giving love. This sixteenth showing reveals in turn that there is within the human heart a similar place so 'large as it were an endless world', which is the soul. In a slight variation to the earlier vision, the sixteenth showing makes it explicit that this place within is a kingdom, thereby echoing the scriptural words of Jesus:

> Now when He was asked by the Pharisees when the kingdom of God would come, He answered them and said, 'The kingdom of God does not come with observation; nor will they say, "See here!" or "See there!" For indeed, the kingdom of God is within you.'
>
> LUKE 17:20–21 (NKJV)

Just as there is a heavenly kingdom which is made accessible to the sinner through the cloven heart of Christ and is the place where those who will be saved can find rest and peace, so there is a kingdom within the heart of the sinner in which Christ is enthroned as Lord and God.

During the 14th century the idea of the kingdom took on a distinct moral understanding, which we can see in the poem *Piers Plowman* by William Langland. Langland's epic account of the soul's journey to find Piers, the figure of Christ, has often been described as vernacular theology, and it gives us a good insight into the theological ideas that were prevalent at the time and how they were expressed. In Book 5 we find an account of the pilgrimage one must take to find the mansion of Truth deep within the soul. The book begins with the dreamer falling asleep and dreaming of the personified figure of Reason, who preaches to the crowd of folk, rousing them to repentance. After each of the seven deadly sins have made their confession, Reason prays to Christ for their forgiveness. The people then set out in search of Truth, but they soon lose their way until Piers the Plowman speaks up from among the crowd and tells them that he knows the path to Truth. He goes on to describe this journey as a pilgrimage, taking them through a figurative pastoral landscape where streams, fords, farms and hills represent the virtues of Meekness, Conscience and the ten commandments. Eventually they will come to a castle, surrounded by the moat of Mercy, with walls of Wisdom and roofed with Love. The doorkeeper is Grace and the password Penance. Once amendment has been entreated, Grace may…

> … give you leave to enter by this gate and there you will find Truth dwelling in your heart, hung on a chain of charity. And you will submit to Him as a child to its father never opposing His will.

For some the pilgrimage to Truth sounds too difficult and they desert Piers returning to their own ways.

In this episode, early on in his poem, Langland gives us a powerful lesson into how a person is to find the palace of Truth within, which is along the road of virtue, obedience and penance. Julian's vision also speaks of a courtly kingdom within where Christ can be found, but for Julian the road to this kingdom is not so much a moral one but a revelatory one. Julian's vision reveals how things are rather than how we experience them to be in this life with all the distortions and distractions of sin. The culmination of Julian's pilgrimage through her showings is not to arrive at a mansion of virtue through attainment, but to look deep within the heart and find there the Lord Jesus Christ already enthroned in the heavenly city of the new Jerusalem. This truth is not to be won but to be simply realised.

The city of God

Since ancient times the image of the city has been used to represent the place of the ultimate ordering of humanity. As opposed to the unpredictability and chaos of the natural order, the city often illustrated the ideal culmination of the aspiration of human civilisation, where people were no longer reliant on agriculture but came together into urban centres that enabled trade and economic stability to thrive, built on surplus food production for all. It allowed for the different professions to flourish, care for the most vulnerable members of the community, artistic expression of the human imagination and the mind to explore new thoughts and ideas. It was seen as the utopia of human living, which existed more as an ideal rather than a place, as beautifully expressed in Thomas More's use of the Greek word for 'no place' to describe his vision of the perfect society. While our experience of the city today may be very different from that painted by the ideal, and more often it is to nature that we yearn to retreat and find ourselves, this image of the city still shapes our visual and theological understanding of the perfect kingdom and realm of God.

The ultimate biblical vision of the city of God is presented in the book of Revelation, which concludes the Bible's journey of salvation that began in Genesis with a perfect garden. Revelation culminates in a vision of God's ultimate social ordering of humanity into the community of the faithful in the new Jerusalem. Here there is still a garden watered by the river of life, which flows from the throne of God and the Lamb, and where the leaves of the tree of life bring healing to the nations, but this garden dwells within the city of God and emanates from the place where he abides within the temple of the soul:

> Now I saw a new heaven and a new earth, for the first heaven and the first earth had passed away. Also there was no more sea. Then I, John, saw the holy city, New Jerusalem, coming down out of heaven from God, prepared as a bride adorned for her husband. And I heard a loud voice from heaven saying, 'Behold, the tabernacle of God is with men, and He will dwell with them, and they shall be His people. God Himself will be with them and be their God. And God will wipe away every tear from their eyes; there shall be no more death, nor sorrow, nor crying. There shall be no more pain, for the former things have

passed away.' Then He who sat on the throne said, 'Behold, I make all things new.' And He said to me, 'Write, for these words are true and faithful.'

REVELATION 21:1–5 (NKJV)

This profound and well-known image is possibly based on Psalm 46, where the psalmist gives words of comfort to the people with a vision of the city of God:

There is a river whose streams make glad the city of God, the holy place where the Most High dwells. God is within her, she will not fall; God will help her at break of day.

PSALM 46:4–5

John uses the same idea of the city as the ultimate vision of salvation where the relationship between humanity and God is restored.

In the stunning Trinity Apocalypse manuscript, dating from the 13th century, the artist precisely presents this biblical passage from the book of Revelation with an image of the outer walls of the city of the new Jerusalem as if it has just descended to the earth through a cloud. John's gaze is not focused on the heavenly building but rather on the mandorla to the side, in which is seen an image of the Lord seated on his throne. John scribbles away capturing the words which the Lord speaks and presents to him (see Plate 9).

The book of Revelation goes on to describe this city in detail, with twelve gates, one for each of the twelve tribes of Israel and three gates on each of the points of the compass. The foundation stones are the twelve apostles and in the centre of the city is the Lord, God Almighty and the Lamb. In the next illumination, in the Trinity Apocalypse manuscript, the artist has again sought to stay true to the biblical narrative and presented the gates and walls of the city in flat-pack style on the page. But the text has moved on as we gaze on the vision of God seated on his throne at the heart of the city, from under which flows the river of the water of life. Seated on his mercy seat the Lord God Almighty raises his hand in blessing while the other rests on an open book which reads 'Amen'. Beside him stands the Lamb of God with a nimbus encircling his head, looking up lovingly into the Lord's face which is presented in a more serious and regal manner than the previous image. In this meditative image, which closely follows the biblical words of John, it is clear that the city represents the restoration of humanity's relationship with God through the enthronement of the Lord God and Christ the Lamb in the heart of the city of the soul. Waters flow once more, but now they are the healing rivers of reconciliation and recreation (see Plate 10).

Julian presents a similar vision of the culmination of the work of salvation at the end of her example of a lord and a servant in chapter 51. Here, the Son sits on the Father's right side in endless rest and peace:

> Now sits the Son, very God and man, in his city in rest and peace, which the Father has prepared for him through his eternal purpose; and the Father in the Son, and the Holy Spirit in the Father and in the Son.

Julian is very careful about her language and tells the reader not to take any of her images literally, unlike Margery Kempe, who presents her Trinitarian understanding of God within the heart of the soul in very visual terms. Margery imagines that her soul is so large that the whole court of heaven can gather there. She decks this chamber with fair flowers and sweet spices and lays out three cushions: one in gold, another of red velvet and a third of white silk, where the Trinity may be worshipped and adored. Much like the Toulouse Apocalypse, Margery includes a remembrance of the passion in the colour of the cushion upon which the Son is to be seated – it is red to denote the passion. In her vision, Christ promises Margery that 'if you allow me, daughter, to rest in your soul on earth, believe it indeed that you shall rest with me in heaven without end'. Margery makes this mutual indwelling as an explicit promise from God to those who love him. Similarly, Julian's vision of Christ enthroned within the city of the soul also mirrors the place where all will be safe within the wounds of his passion. But Julian does not see a vision of the Trinity or even one of the Lord and the Lamb; rather her vision is of the person of Christ enthroned as Lord and God.

Lord Jesus Christ

Throughout the visions of salvation, from the tenth showing onwards, Christ has been speaking to Julian, responding to her questions and asking his own. This has been an intimate conversation which has allowed for doubts and inner concerns to be expressed by Julian, especially around his words that 'all shall be well'. Now he makes an appearance, but this is not an intimate showing of Jesus as the lover; rather it is as a person of great stature and reverence. The three titles given to him – 'highest bishop, noblest king and honourable lord' – emphasise the awe and respect which Christ commands, as well as his authority in the spiritual, temporal and feudal realms on earth. In these honours Julian reminds us that while ordinary people live under the authority of these institutions, it is God the Trinity who holds ultimate dominion over the whole realm of heaven and earth through the person of Christ. It is he who invests these institutions with their authority; they do not hold it of themselves.

This sixteenth vision not only culminates the journey of the sixteen showings to a vision of salvation, it also incorporates many of the ideas and specific language that Julian has used within those former showings. This can especially be revealed in her description of Christ. As we have seen, Julian not only picks up the language of the Son sitting in his city in rest and peace from the example of a lord and a servant in chapter 51, she also refers back to this exemplum in the very same words she uses to describe Christ's robes and the manner in which he is 'solemnly and worshipfully clad'. After the initial visionary unfolding of the example in chapter 51, Christ tells Julian to deeply contemplate the significance of the many aspects which she sees, the clothes that the lord and servant wear and their colour being not the least of these. As Julian reflects on these robes it soon becomes clear that the garments the lord and the servant wear are at various times visual markers of the effect of sin and the work of Christ.

Julian begins by considering the robe and situation of the lord. Initially he is seen as sitting in a simple place, barren and desert, alone in the wilderness. Though, we are told, he made man's soul to be his own city and dwelling place, due to the fall it is no longer able to perform this noble office. So, the lord sits in a barren desert and waits for the time when Christ the servant redeems his city by his hard labour on the cross and makes it once more the place of noble beauty where the lord may rest. The lord's clothing is described as being wide and ample, which is seemly for a lord, and blue in colour. Julian explains that the blue of the clothing betokens his steadfastness, and the fullness reveals that he has enclosed within himself all heavens. Like Christ in the sixteenth vision, he is fair and most seemly, and looks on the fallen servant with love and pity.

In contrast, the robe of the servant is a white, old, unlined and worn-out tunic, streaked with sweat and tattered by the thorns and nails of the passion. This is the robe of Adam, which Christ the servant clothes himself with in order to take on the sin of the servant Adam. The exemplum concludes with a vision of reconciliation as the servant stands before the lord, but now the tattered robes of Adam are newly made and he wears a beautiful robe, which is white and bright and of endless purity, full and flowing, fairer and richer than that on the lord. While the lord's garment is blue, Christ the servant's is a marvellous mixture of light which is truly more glorious.

The significance of the robes of the lord and the servant to reflect their nature, work and property is continued into the sixteenth vision. Here Christ is depicted neither as the servant with a tattered tunic or robes of light, nor as the lord with garments of blue steadfastness. Instead, Julian sees him as solemnly and worshipfully clad as befits our Lord Jesus Christ. He wears robes which express his authority as the Lord but also the glorious robes of the Son. Julian has brought together in one person the figure of the Lord and the Servant Christ.

We have seen this Trinitarian reference throughout the revelations. But perhaps this image is most closely associated with the first showing, where Julian looked upon Christ on the cross and saw there that the whole Trinity was present. In the same way, she now looks on the enthroned Christ and realises that 'the Godhead rules and takes care of heaven and earth and all that is, sovereign might, sovereign wisdom, and sovereign goodness'. Each aspect of his authority represents a property of the Trinity: the might of the Father, the wisdom of the Son and the goodness of the Holy Spirit. Even as Julian gazed on the suffering of Christ on the cross, her heart was suddenly filled with heavenly joy as she realises that within Christ the Trinity is present, within even the suffering of Christ the joy and peace of the Trinity is found.

Julian sees that the work of the Trinity is in and through his properties of being our maker, our keeper and our everlasting lover and it is through the Trinity, dwelling deep within the heart, that the soul finds endless joy and bliss by our Lord Jesus Christ. Now in the culmination of her visions, Julian sees the reality of the presence of the Trinity deep within us through Christ so that no matter what happens, however bad or destructive sin may be, however much this may be forgotten or the mire of this world dim our vision, the Lord Jesus Christ is enthroned there, giving rest and peace. So, Julian's eyes have been turned from contemplating the suffering and sin of this external world to the truth of the presence of God within the city of the soul.

At the end of the vision Julian once again heard Jesus speaking to her. But just as in the previous times she received his words but did not hear his voice or see his lips move, so now his counsel comes to her for the last time:

Know it well that it was no raving which you had this day; but receive it and believe it and hold on to it; keep and comfort yourself withal and trust in it, and thereby you shall not be overcome.

In these words, Julian is not only reassured that her revelation is true but also is given words of comfort and strength going forward. As she ponders what Jesus has said, she realises that he did not say, 'You shall not be tempted, you shall not be troubled, you shall not be distressed', but he said, 'You shall not be overcome.' So, Julian's revelations come to a close and she sees no more.

The Devil comes again with his heat and vile stench. He mocks her prayers, babbling with his beads and tries to stir her to despair. But this time she sets her eyes upon the crucifix, the very same from which the showings emerged, and she rehearses the passion of Christ and recalls her faith in the 'holy church'. And so she scorns the Devil, and he is overcome. Just as Christ had said, in *wele* and woe we are ever kept saved, loved and pleasing in his sight, and so it is in this revelation of the truth that Julian and we must trust, and then indeed we shall truly believe without knowing that all shall be well.

─────── *Going deeper* ───────

Give yourself time to linger on these words by Julian:

The place that Jesus takes in our soul, he shall never be removed from without end as to my sight; for in us is his homeliest home and his endless dwelling.

What do these words say to you?

What do you find challenging and why?

What do you think Jesus would like to say to you?

Allow your time of thinking and reflection to lead you into a deeper place of prayer and love.

What will you take away with you from this time of meditation?

Questions to ponder

- What have these visions of salvation shown to you?
- What has surprised you about them and what have you found difficult?
- What meaning does the word 'salvation' have for you?
- How can we live as people who are safe or saved?

Words for the journey

Those who love me will keep my word, and my Father will love them, and we will come to them and make our home with them.

JOHN 14:23 (NRSV)

CONCLUSION

I step down into the inviting space which is the reconstructed anchorhold of Julian at Norwich. I am alone and it pulsates with a silence I fear to disturb. No one comes.

There is a bowl of hazelnuts on the side as you enter and for a moment I look at it scornfully as another misrepresentation of Julian's words. For once, though, I put my arrogance in my pocket and pick one up. It is smooth and hard, rolling around in my fingers as I play with this little thing as small as a ball. For a moment I think I will pray, but I am alone and drop the pretence. Instead, I just sit, sit in the silence, nonchalantly playing with my hazelnut that fixes my attention in a dreamlike, focused way.

I try to imagine Julian being in this space, but I can't. I try to remember her words, but they elude me. Instead, I simply sit, caressing the nut that lies in the palm of my hand. No one comes. I am alone. It is time to leave, and with great effort I pull myself away, ever glancing back towards the door as I leave the empty church.

Months later and the little hazelnut has become part of my cassock pocket. It rolls around in its universe of darkness. Occasionally I remember it's there but mostly not. Until one day I meet a visitor to the cathedral. She tells me about her friend who is seriously ill and how she has found comfort and solace in Julian's words:

> All shall be well, and all shall be well, and all manner of thing shall be well.

It was those words which gave her friend, in the midst of her terminal illness, a sense of hope and deep peace. She spoke of the hazelnuts that filled a bowl at the Julian shrine and how she wished she had one to give to her friend. In a moment of unthinking spontaneity, I reached into my pocket and groped about in its blackness until my fingers once again clasped the little ball, the size of a hazelnut, and gave it to her. Her eyes filled with astounded tears as I overcame her attempts not to receive my gift. But she knew that this was not about giving or receiving, it was a moment over which neither of us had any power.

I do not know whether 'all shall be well'. Like Julian I grapple intellectually, spiritually and emotionally with these words, those hopes in a secret deed, a present assurance that I have seen give comfort and profound trust in others. Their testaments and witness to faith profoundly move me where my suffering and the pain I feel for the state of our world leave me only with the cry: 'How can all things be well?'

A few months later a strange envelope alights on our doormat. The paper is hardly able to hold what it contains. I gingerly open this strange missive and fumble around inside until I discover a little thing hiding in the white corner. It is a hazelnut. A postcard from the Julian anchorhold is enclosed and it simply reads, 'Thank you.' My heart was cloven in two, and I wept at the profound simplicity and beauty of such a gift, freely and lovingly given.

Julian never really resolves her questioning or understanding of Jesus' words. Perhaps that is where they should lie, within the mystery of God's being and the compassion of his work in people's lives. Instead, she looks beyond this little world, loved, created and held by God, and makes Christ's words her own. Beyond the veil, in the silence of being, a gift is given:

> And then shall none of us be stirred to say in anything: 'Lord, if it had been thus, it had been well.' But we shall all say with

one voice: 'Lord, blessed must this be, for it is thus, it is well. And now we see truly that all things are done as it was thine ordinance, before anything was made.'

And the hazelnut?

It rolls around once more in my cassock pocket reminding me that indeed, all can be well, all may be well, and all manner of things shall be well.

FURTHER READING

Revelations of Divine Love, editions and translations

Julian of Norwich: Showings, edited and translated by Edmund Colledge and
James Walsh, Classics of Western Spirituality Series (Paulist Press, 1978).
The Showings of Julian of Norwich, edited by Denise N. Baker, Norton Critical
Edition (W.W. Norton & Co., 2005).
A Revelation of Divine Love, edited by Marion Glasscoe (Exeter University Press,
1986).
The Complete Julian of Norwich, translated by Fr. John-Julian, Paraclete Giants
Series (Paraclete Press, 2009).
*The Writings of Julian of Norwich: A vision showed to a devout woman and
a revelation of love*, edited by Nicholas Watson and Jaqueline Jenkins (The
Pennsylvania State University Press, 2006).
Julian of Norwich: Revelations of Divine Love, edited by Barry Windeatt (Oxford
University Press, 2016).

Studies in Julian

Abbot, Christopher, *Julian of Norwich: Autobiography and theology* (D.S. Brewer,
1999).
Baker, Denise, *Julian of Norwich's Showings: From vision to book* (Princeton
University Press, 1994).
Fox, Matthew, *Julian of Norwich: Wisdom in a time of pandemic – and beyond*
(iUniverse, 2020).
Fruehwirth, Robert, *The Drawing of This Love: Growing in faith with Julian of
Norwich* (Canterbury Press, 2016).
Glasscoe, Marion, *English Medieval Mystics: Games of faith* (Longman, 1993).
Jantzen, Grace M., *Julian of Norwich: Mystic and theologian* (SPCK, 2011).
Llewelyn, Robert (ed.), Julian: Woman of our day (Darton, Longman and Todd, 1985).
Llewelyn, Robert, *With Pity Not With Blame: Reflections on the writings of Julian of*

Norwich and on The Cloud of Unknowing (Darton, Longman and Todd, 1982).

Nuth, Joan, *Wisdom's Daughter: The theology of Julian of Norwich* (Crossroad, 1997).

Pennington, Emma, *At the Foot of the Cross with Julian of Norwich* (BRF Ministries, 2020).

Ramirez, Janina, *Julian of Norwich: a very brief history* (SPCK, 2016).

Rolf, Veronica Mary, *Julian's Gospel: Illuminating the life and revelations of Julian of Norwich* (Orbis Books, 2013).

Sheldrake, Philip, *Julian of Norwich: In God's sight – her theology in context* (Wiley Blackwell, 2018).

Turner, Denys, *Julian of Norwich, Theologian* (Yale University Press, 2011).

Upjohn, Shelia, *Why Julian Now? A voyage of discovery* (Friends of Julian of Norwich, 2014).

Ward, Sr. Benedicta, 'Julian the solitary', in Kenneth Leech, *Julian Reconsidered* (SLG Press, 1988).

Praying with Julian

Durka, Gloria, *Praying with Julian*, Companions for the Journey Series (Saint Mary's Press, 2001).

de Gruchy, Isobel, *Making All Things Well: Finding spiritual strength with Julian of Norwich* (Paulist Press, 2013).

Lewin, Ann, *Love is the Meaning: Growing in faith with Julian of Norwich* (Canterbury Press, 2006).

Nelson, John, *Julian of Norwich: Journeys into joy: selected spiritual writings* (New City Press, 2001).

Upjohn, Shelia, *The Way of Julian of Norwich: A prayer journey through Lent* (SPCK, 2020).

Novels about Julian

Coles, Margaret, *The Greening* (Hay House, 2013).

Gilbert, Claire, *I, Julian* (Hodder and Stoughton, 2023).

Mackenzie, Victoria, *For Thy Great Pain Have Mercy on My Little Pain* (Bloomsbury, 2023).

Parke, Simon, *The Secret Testament of Julian* (White Crow Books, 2018).

BRF Ministries

Inspiring people of all ages to grow in Christian faith

BRF Ministries is the home of Anna Chaplaincy, Living Faith, Messy Church and Parenting for Faith

As a charity, our work would not be possible without fundraising and gifts in wills.
To find out more and to donate,
visit brf.org.uk/give or call +44 (0)1235 462305